The Com·pos·men·tis

Written by:
Michael W. Bryant

Cadmus Publishing
www.cadmuspublishing.com

Copyright © 2022 Michael W. Bryant

Published by Cadmus Publishing
www.cadmuspublishing.com
Port Angeles, WA

ISBN: 978-1-63751-123-7
Library of Congress Control Number: 2022900811

All rights reserved. Copyright under Berne Copyright Convention, Universal Copyright Convention, and Pan-American Copyright Convention. No part of this book may be reproduced, stored in a retrieval system, or transmitted in any form, or by any means, electronic, mechanical, photocopying, recording or otherwise, without prior permission of the author.

Preface

Welcome to Com.pos.men.tis. I would like to give thanks to the prison's Foundation for giving me this opportunity to share my literary work with the world. The poems you are about to embark upon are the result of my life struggles, trials, and tribulations, but as you read them you will learn that even in the heart of chaos, something good can rise up. By far this is the best part of me and my token to the world. So, I hope that you will gain something from them that will benefit everyone on their life journey. I look forward to any and all comments, so feel free to contact me by the address below or log onto JPay.com and send me your emails.

Sincerely,

Michael Bryant #1066161
Augusta Correctional Center
1821 Estaline Valley Road
Craigsville, VA 24430

In Loving Memory

…of my mother,
Laura Jean Wilson-Bryant

Dedications

With my deepest gratitude to my father, Roosevelt Jr., my brother Roosevelt III, my sister Melissa, my aunt Shirley and Angie for your love and support.

Acknowledgements

I would like to thank the Theosophical Society, Syda Yoga Foundation, The Prison Foundation and the late Dr. Mike of Promise Ministries. You all helped me find the knowledge and understanding of self that brought about the wisdom to apply it towards the writing of this once-in-a-lifetime-book, The Composmentis.

Special Mention

To the artist Calvin Williams in taking my thoughts for this book cover and bringing it to life in this drawing.

Thank you.

Introduction

This book is not your ordinary poetry book, nor is it like any book you've ever read. It touches on all aspects of life with a universal reality that will make you second-guess your own reality and think outside the box.

We believe that we are defined by our trials and tribulations. The truth is that it is not what we go through, but what we learn form it. These poems are nothing more than a collaboration of experiences formulated to stimulate a spiritual awakening in the reader.

So, buckle up, because you are about to embark on one hell of a ride to the mental side of my world, that I know you will enjoy!

Contents

The Pen and Paper	1
Who Am I	3
Birds	4
Water Falls	5
The Ark of the Covenant	6
Mad Thoughts	7
Love Is	8
The Verdict	9
Dear Momma	11
It's A Beautiful Thing	12
Elixir, the Mental Fixer	14
Priceless	16
Color Blind	17
In The Fit of Rage	19
A Vintage in the Making	20
New Year	21
Bars, Windows, and Handcuffs	22
The Thoughtless	25
Victims of the System	26
Poetry Is	27
Willpower	28
The Chemistry	29
Broken Glass	30
Day Dreaming	31
Potential	32
The Energy Theory	33
Whoever Said	35
Time	36
Soldiers	37
The Man Behind The Mirror	38
Life Amazing	39
Sam I Am	40
Prison Blues	41
Irony	42
True Fact	43
Where's The Love	44
When I Die	45
Fear The Darkness	46
My Analysis	47
Spring Again!	48
Dazed and Confused	49
The Inner Self Apocalypse	50
Me and the Cat in the Tree	51
The Butterfly Effect	52
I See You	53
Yesterday, Today and Tomorrow	54
My Window	55
Dilemma	56

Shake It Off	60
Else-Where	61
A Lifetime	62
If Only For A Moment	63
The Scale of Justice	64
Problems	65
One Extraordinary Day	66
The Recipe For Poetry	67
I Trusted You	68
This Old House	69
Taking Nothing for Granted	71
More Than Flesh and Bones	72
Rainbows	73
The Vow	74
Masquerade	75
Lies	76
The Flim-Flam	77
Just A Dream	78
I Wonder	79
Racist	80
Faces	81
Serene	82
Diversity	83
Revenge	84
What's the Value of Life?	85
Ghost Writer	87
To Be or Not to Be	88
Beat The Drum	89
Drama Is	90
Spontaneous	91
Here Today, Gone Tomorrow	92
True Friends	93
The Scenario	94
Throw Away People	95
My Sanctuary	96
Pure Adrenaline	97
Bonafide	98
Tempo	99
Progress	100
Exclusive	101
The Struggle	102
Dear America	103
The Tree of Life	106
Rain	107
Problematic	109
Planet Earth	110
Zenith	111
Just A Drop	112
I Just Cry About It	113
Flick of the Switch	114
Imagine This	115
The Cabin in the Woods	116

Reminiscence	117
Stripped	118
Hear Ye, Hear Ye	119
Determination	120
My Finale	121
Smoke	122
We Don't Exist	123
The Poetic Master	124
Stagnation	125
The In Between	126
A Passing Thought	127
A Year	128
Outside The Box	129
Kundalini	130
So Tired	131
The Simple Life	132
Anything	133
Change	134
Anonymous	135
Blissness	136
Been Around the World	137
Suicidal Tendencies	138
Can We Come Together	139
Breath After Breath	141
The Seed Trilogy	142
A Dangerous Mind	143
Queen Bee	144
The THEOREM	145
I Don't Want	146
Never Been In Love	147
The Human Odyssey	148
I Cry	149
Anticipation	150
Devil	151
Self-Inflicted	152
Technical Difficulties	153
Kiss the Sky	154
Life	155
Words of Wisdom	156
Some Time This, Some Time That	157
When My Eyes Close	158
Love Is Pt. 2	159
Change Pt. 2	160
"The City of the Dead"	161
A Ghost of a Man	164
Memories	165
The Grit and the Grind	166
Give Me The Strength	167
A Second Class Citizen	168
The Most Beauteous Thing	169
The Supreme	170
No Discipline	171

Title	Page
Just Anybody	172
Retrospect	173
The Journey Within	174
I Know Your Struggle	175
Soul Anthem	177
Remember The Times	179
The Humanimal Kingdom	182
Our Father	183
Listen Up	186
The Visionary	187
Desperado	189
When Sunshine Turns To Rain	190
Sensory	192
Greatness	193
You Are	194
A Matter Of Opinion	195
Autumn Breeze	196
Flawless	197
The Hustle Of A Lifetime	198
The Life of a Clown	199
We	200
Rude Awakening	201
Never Free	202
Divide and Conquer	203
NoneTheLess	204
The Seven Levels of Consciousness	205
Day After Day	206
The Crime Scene	207
Real Men Cry, Too	210
Aging Gracefully	212
I Am Not Just A Man	214
Tears	216
My Definition of Music	218
Dazzled By A Poet	220
I AM	222
Flame On Me	224
The Forces That Be	226
The Transition	228
Rejuvenation	231
IF	232
I Need A Woman	235
The Death of a Flower	236
The Pen and Paper Part 2	237
Saying Goodbye	239
No Proof of Life	240
Wake Up	241
The Crime	242
Promises	243
Rhythm of the Rhyme	244
I Remember Now	245

The Pen and Paper

It's something special about the pen,
and the way it feels when I grip it time
and time again.
Also, don't forget about the paper which
soaks up the ink and every word that I
can think.
I keep both of them close like my next
of kin, it's nothing like having two best
friends.
They allow me to speak freely without any
unnecessary discrepancies such as if's,
and's, and maybe's.
They respect my profession without any
questions and I have an unlimited amount
of discretion.
I'm able to speak with the ink, line after
line about what's on my mind.
For me it's the greatest therapy, because
I'm totally free to write out my own destiny.
In my heart lies a great desire to
inspire that burns like fire, and like
any religion, I'm envisioned with a mission
like a chef in a kitchen mixing and fixing.
My forte is fortitude which I use
to elude the mind with something
different, not just dreams and memories,
but something that will last for
centuries.
So, let me take your mind on the ultimate
ride to a whole new world with streets
made out of diamonds and pearls.
Where birds don't fly,
but walk among the tree tops and where
love is eternal like a tunnel that never

stops, but runs so deep it's beyond reality.
As I read from the podium, my words
be flowing out of my mouth and off of
my lips like water over a cliff.
So, relax, lay back and listen
for my words will massage and soothe
your mind like a fine wine.
In time you will all see that through
my words you already know me.
Unlike an artist who paints pictures,
I paint words that will get you in tune
with me and the things I see.
I thank the Almighty for this gift
to uplift other people, it's like magic
out of a situation so tragic was
born something so fantastic and everlasting.
Without a question it's the power of expression
that is no longer deceased, giving me the
ability to release something so delicately
with sincerity.
I don't know what it is, but I hold it
tight all through the night,
it's my greatest love and the paper
is no longer white, but pinstripe
as the ink glistens in the moonlight.
Even in the dark I can see the words
popping out of my head onto the walls
dancing and romancing my mind
with new ideas to write and recite
to those with ears.

Who Am I

I am the good,
the bad, the happy,
the sad, the rich, the
poor, the successful, the
regretful, the criminal,
the thug, the crooked politician
sweeping justice beneath the rug,
the nice fellow, the bank teller,
the drug dealer with buried
money in the cellar, the murderer,
the minister, the sinister, the lover,
the hater, the procrastinator,
the sick, the feeble, the wicked,
the evil, the dangerous, the
strangest individual you
will ever meet, the one who
will kill you in your sleep, the
humble, the meek, the living,
the dead, it's one of the same,
I'm everything, so who am I,
just one multiplied.

May 5, 2015

Birds

They fly among the clouds
with little effort
and float down like leaves
from heaven as they cling
to the winds like a mother
to her child making you smile.
From eagles to hummingbirds
they all travel across the world.
They're amazing in every
shape and size with those
mystic, pearl-black eyes,
captivating me with their
many colors and their style
is like no other.
They live in all trees
in any degrees for God
tends their every need.
Oh, how beautiful it must
be just to fly free!

March 15, 2012

Water Falls

Oceans,
Seas,
And
Rivers
deliver great lakes
of
streams, creeks and ponds
too much to look upon
as the rain continue
to make rushing waters
from on high
come
crashing down from the sky
with that oh, so familiar
sound just before hitting,
the ground.

March 2, 2012

The Ark of the Covenant

(1) My astrological sign
    is one of the divine,
        twelve in all when combined.
(2) My element is of fire.
    A trio, Sagittarius,
        Aries, and Leo.
(3) My soul is a spark
    from the Ark of the Covenant.
(4) The greater my intensities,
    the greater my desire to rise
        rapidly and gloriously.
(5) I have no limitations
    for I am consumed by
        God's revelation.
(6) Out of the ashes
    I rose like the phoenix,
        eyes gleaming with small
            flames of passion screaming.
(7) Drops of my vitality
    sizzle as it hits the ground,
        telling the universe that another
            soul has touched down.

November 23, 2014

Mad Thoughts

Each day is a hellish nightmare,
  causing me to sit and stare into
    space as I think to myself what a
    waste.
I have no hope or faith and this
  Life I can no longer take.
Suicide was my first thought, but I
  didn't have the heart.
Then, I blamed God for my pain
  that's when I knew I was going
    insane.
I feel like an animal locked in a
  cage, crushed by the pressure of my
    own rage.
Yet, I created this drama for myself
  and had the nerve to blame someone
    else, but this is what
      "mad thoughts" do, confuse you.

October 1, 2006

Love Is

Love is
the passion that burns
in God's heart, the light
that came forth from
the dark, the reason
the universe came to be
that gave birth to the
earth then humanity.
The ruler of all dimensions
from start to finish,
love is love with no competition,
definition unlimited
a face with no description,
the key to all states of
realities, the seed in reasoning
and the power of hope in believing,
that's what love is and
the greater it will be
throughout
infinity.

May 11, 2015

The Verdict

I stand
accused of a crime,
murder in the first degree
and if convicted, I face the
death penalty.
 The media has already
convicted me in the public
eye of society with no sympathy,
that's why I smile and stay
strong for my family, but these
court deliberations is mentally
draining while the prosecutor
continue with the psychological
framing.
   A capital offense.
   means two lawyers for my
   defense and although I am
   innocent, my fight is diligent
   like a militant.
     So, just in case I'm
     found guilty, this is for
     the jury. A jury of my peers,
     but what if I'm actually
     innocent, shouldn't that
     be your worst fears.
        While the twelve of you
        are faced with a tedious
        mission based on the
        evidence presented to make
        a hell of a decision. Life,
        death, guilty or not guilty.
          The innocent don't always

go free and sometime the guilty get the not guilty.

    With my life hanging in the balance, let my words be more than just a conscious challenge, but a spiritual test within yourself before you convict, because there's no turning back once you render the verdict.

April 16, 2015

Dear Momma

When
our eyes met on that very day it was a
miracle in every way up to and beyond
the month of May. But since this is the
day set aside and recognized that
means one more to realize three
hundred and sixty-five that
you're still alive as my love
for you will never die, words
can't explain the way I
feel about you and all of
the things you still do
with a love for me that
has always been
loyal and true.
You held my hand
when I was a child as
you watched me grow into
a man and even though I'm grown
now I can still feel your touch
that's why I love you so very much
because you never let go and as we
continue this journey together along
the way, I just had to stop and say…

Happy Mother's Day!

May 14, 2015

MICHAEL WAYNE BRYANT

It's A Beautiful Thing

A combination of both genders
the yin and the yang brought
together with one aim. A process
not defined by who's greater,
both becoming equal creators.
A moment when time completely
stops to adopt a show of its
gratitude towards humanity
the cream of the crops, as if to
hold its breath and watch the hands
on a clock. Then, suddenly one sperm
out of millions has reached its
designation without complication in
the fertilization of a female egg to
bring forth a manifestation called
creation upon this great plantation that was said to be
      last in God's creation
is now first, bursting forth like soldiers
in war. Not to die, but to multiply.

      As the flesh of your
flesh to come forth and take one breath
of life is like a slice of destiny divided
by ecstasy. Speaking of you
and me becoming entwined in
something so holy and divine.
To bring forth flesh, bones and
skin while going within to formulate
muscles, ligaments, tendons and
tissue with no ending as it starts
mending and blending our DNA.
Calculating along the way every

aspect of our existence with precision until its finish. Finally, a mirror reflection of self, a creation like nothing else from you and me to create something so beautiful called a baby!

Elixir, the Mental Fixer

(1) I have no license
nor the qualification
to hand out medication,
but the elixir is the
mental fixer,
not a drug, so I don't need
certification.
(2) So, if you take a sip
it's at your own risk.
Even then death is less
than one-fifth equal
the rest in total bliss.
(3) From the physical to the
spiritual to a superconscious
state of mind to a place
not governed by space or time.
A whole new terrain
within the brain that
not even a physicist can
explain.
(4) Where you don't eat, breathe,
or sleep and how you exist
is a scientific mystery.
(5) The scenery is so dreamy
it's unimaginable and
the greenery illuminates the
eyes making everything
tangible.
(6) The scent of lavender hangs
in the air like chandeliers,
as sheer blue skies reflect
past memories by the years.

(7) Crystal clear waters
shimmer with the all so fine
precious metals known
to mankind in a world
that only lasted for a short
period of time.
(8) This, my friends, is better
than any wine, it's
elixir time!

December 6, 2014

Priceless

I can't say enough
about how important Living is
and giving is.
For every single day,
I take a moment of silence
to get away from the world
of corruption and violence just
to welcome the sun with a smile
on my face, giving thanks
to God for creating such a
beautiful place.
Yearning for its beauty
like the birds that nest
in the trees as I hunger
for the opportunity to live
out my destiny.
For if I could, I would
bottle up all of my experiences and might
Just, nah I couldn't
It's priceless!

October 2, 2006

Color Blind

More than ever
we base life on what we see,
but that's not possible for
me.
Fifty shades of gray
is not my reality,
but more like one shade
of gray with no duality.
No color, that means no
red, no blue, no green, or
yellow.
A condition since birth,
but I still enjoy life for
all that it's worth.
Never been a racist,
nor could I ever be, and
that's the truth
signed sincerely.
In my world,
all I see is figures
called bodies moving around
me, the silhouettes of humanity.
So, what's your excuse
for feeling the way you do.
What's the reason
for you hating him or
him hating you.
You never been associates
or friends, so where
did it all begin.
Passed on from the next of
kin to the next of kin,

when will it end.
Being color blind is
more of a blessing,
not a defect,
but a lesson.
So, I despise
those who haven't realized
the value of life
over color.
If this is considered
normal behavior,
I would have rather
died during labor.

March 8, 2015

In The Fit of Rage

In split seconds,
  your blood pressure will rise
    giving you bloodshot eyes
      causing sweat to pour from
        your face. then your breathing
          becomes displaced as your
          hands begin to shake.
         This is the effects of anger
        when it over-take, then
       suddenly violence takes place just
      before realizing that you made a
    grave mistake, because hindsight
  is always too little too late.

February 8, 2007

A Vintage in the Making

Antiques
 are something people keep,
but what about the words
 we speak that seep into
our consciousness as we sleep.
A pedigree of seeds planted
 into our minds that
   grow like grapes on a
     vine, manifesting mental
       pictures of all kinds.
Fast forward, stop, now play,
 then rewind as syllables
   drop into formation to
     form words into sentences
       called communication.
Simply exquisite and divine
 with only a glimpse
   of a vintage in time.

May 9, 2015

New Year

A New Year
brings new opportunities,
goals and dedication without
past stipulations.
Some say it's
Just another day,
which is true, but it's
also a chance to start something
new. So, cheers
to you and all that
you do. For
myself, I stand
strong in my belief,
but I always leave room
to turn over a new leaf.
So be all
you can be and have
a Happy New Year from
me.

November 28, 2006

Bars, Windows, and Handcuffs

Bars, windows and handcuffs,
bars, windows, and handcuffs,
as if this wasn't enough!
Bars, windows and handcuffs.
Taking a sip
from a poisonous cup
is like contributing to
your own death, suicide to
your last breath.
Stripped to your bare essentials,
a worthless excuse for a
human being with no potential.
It's elementary
so you don't need a documentary
to see all the misery
throughout penitentiaries.
The mentally deficient,
so many to choose from,
it's like pots and pans
in the kitchen, something
here is terribly missing.
Bars, windows and handcuffs,
bars, windows and handcuffs,
as if this wasn't enough!
Bars, windows and handcuffs.
Try this on for instance.
when waking up is no longer
consistent and
the sound of a whistle
blaring with the
jingling of keys
bring you back to this

*sad reality, with flashlights
smacking you in the face
like giant spotlights
in the middle of the night that
will have you feeling uptight
as you try to regain
your sight, struggling to shake
the sleep and stand on your feet a task
not performed easily.
Move too quick and you
may become dizzy.
Nevertheless,
it's all in vain,
for all that you see
is a couple of shadows
passing the door frame.
Bars, windows and handcuffs,
bars, windows and handcuffs,
as if this wasn't enough!
Bars, windows and handcuffs.
The constant repetition
becomes malicious and
vicious as it starts
attacking your consciousness.
Then you lose focus
slipping away into the
darkness.
The killings and stabbings
are no longer frightening,
nor the beatings or robberies that
become exciting.
You may gamble, drink,
get high, or have sex with
the gay guy 'cause only
the strong will survive,*

*the rest will die
mentally or physically.
Consequently, all of this
should be kept confidential,
the conclusion is no
illusion, it's nothing less
than detrimental.
Bars, windows and handcuffs,
bars, windows and handcuffs,
as if this wasn't enough!
Bars, windows and handcuffs.*

October 10, 2010

The Thoughtless

The thoughtless,
   take oil from your core and always
      looking for more.
The thoughtless,
   dig in your flesh like parasites
      and blow holes in you with dynamite.
The Thoughtless,
   steal and claim your precious metals
      then sale them for a price on sight.
The Thoughtless,
Kill the trees and pollute the air
   with chemicals and toxins
      likes killers for hire
         Just to build buildings
            called empires.
The Thoughtless,
   assassinate the animals of the sea
      and land with weapons of
         violence in their hand.
I'm not flawless
   Nor am I thoughtless,
      but I must live with the shame in
         Knowing that humanity is the blame.

April 1, 2007

Victims of the System

It's a shame
to see so many youths
fall through the cracks this
isn't a movie you can't stop the
reel and rewind life back. A nation
of youths under attack, so many tears
and no turning back. Drugs, alcohol, gang
banging, and throwing up gang signs
while mother's crying 'cause their
son's dying in the streets, bloody
sheets, black bags and toe tags is
what it's going to be and if they
survive it will be in the penitentiary.
This is the system and the youth
are the victims, juvenile
detention no program prevention
so where's the government
intervention. Moms and dads
got to get ironclad and go
the extra mile in raising their child
teach them because the system
won't reach them and the
streets will only beat them
into someone you no longer
recognize, lost in the system
another life jeopardized, victim.

May 30, 2015

Poetry Is

Poetry is
  an ancient art
    formulated to produce
      thoughts from the deepest
        passions of the heart with
          all of the experiences of life
          wrapped into one then
          expressed by words
            until you're done.

August 13, 2007

Willpower

Let your will explode
 like dynamite to ignite
 your determination, where we all lack
patience, hold
strong and face it
 for your will is like a warrior's
shield,
 trained to kill obstacles before they
   have a chance to build
like a piece of steel that
 never bends or breaks, nor pain or
suffering can overtake,
 making the weak strong
and the strong stronger
 in a world where you must
   fight or be conquered.

March 14, 2012

The Chemistry

What is a ministry
without a belief system or a leaf without
the color green,
you know what I mean I'm just speaking
logically and what is life without
goals or ambitions just
another hopeless mission.
Therefore you ask,
what is the chemistry? And I tell you
this even for me it is a mystery,
but is always there as the
air we breathe.
For it is like the wind
with a different blend that blows from
within Beneath the skin that
possess great qualities of
peace and always
in harmony with the fabric of time,
combined to define something
that is neither here nor there,
but everywhere.

July 17, 2007

Broken Glass

Shards of broken glass lie near a
window not yet broken as past
incidents are no longer spoken. Anger
in the form of a fist, consists of a
force upon impact causing the wood
to splinter and crack. While the
window-pane reflection shows
one's perception, muddy waters
become clear when still no
deception. The sound of a violin
symbolizes the pains of life
all over again. Prone to bend
but never to break like glass
for picking up the pieces is
a thing of the past because
emotional ties scatter
like broken glass.

June 21, 2015

Day Dreaming

*Sometime,
when I'm wide awake my
mind just Floats away.
Taking me to places
I've never been and showing
me things I've never
seen.
Oh, how beautiful it
is to dream, suddenly I
caught myself asking, what
just happened!*

February 6, 2008

Potential

The
potential for manifestations
is infinite and
its possibilities are unlimited,
for every star in the universe so are
our choices galloping upon the
planets like wild horses,
turning anything into something and
making space out of nothing,
summoning thoughts out of nothingness
and filling the mind with substance,
the brain cells submit like
hostages as it craves for oxygen,
but the soul holds the key to all
realms of reality, where the flesh
and bones are three dimensional
the truth is solid and impenetrable,
because here lies the greatness
for potential.

June 25, 2015

The Energy Theory

*Out of the abyss
came a mist
so small it could fit
inside a fist,
from a place
in complete darkness
before the universe
was created,
where its birth
can't be estimated
as it formulated itself
into pure matter,
something called an atom.
Then exploded and shattered
sending its particles
into the depths of
complete emptiness to
create a nucleus.
Something we call the
living into existence
with its construction still
pending while bending
its own generated heat
to ignite a substance
called light. Out
of the light came a spark
that turned into a thought
that created a
manifestation called creation,
but creation laid stagnated
until the crafty hands
of pure matter sent*

the atom forth,
letting its nucleus inject
light into creation
giving it simulation
and a source of communication.
Creation then swam
out into the ocean of darkness
to cause something
called motion and motion
brought about
movement to the pure
matter, so it could
construct thoughts
into solid objects
as it traveled.
Even more tremendous
life burst forth
as a living organism
from the core of this
one seed to create
a trilogy of itself
called humanity.

August 28, 2007

Whoever Said

Whoever said,
  there was a heaven and hell
    then died and came back
      to tell.
Whoever said,
  money don't mean a thing,
    you think the poor feel the
      same.
Whoever said,
  to forgive is to forget,
    but who can stop themselves
      from remembering it.
Whoever said,
  food should be free,
    but turn around and
      charge me.
        If I pay then I eat,
      if not, then I go hungry.
Whoever said,
  what I said is true,
    but that is to be judged
      only by you.

December 2, 2007

Time

What is time,
but the hands on a clock
that goes around and around
non-stop.
Never to be held
or even touched,
no not even that much.
Never to be seen with
a face,
color
or shape and can't be
located in one certain place.
Then tell me why,
so many try to defy
time if it's all
in the mind.

February 24, 2010

Soldiers

Soldiers
fight for freedom,
justice, and equality.
They strive to stay alive
and with fear they don't
compromise, shoulder to shoulder
they stand to protect this land.
Whether you care or not, with every
shot a life is lost, but it is the cost that
a soldier pays so you can live free another
day, at home or abroad they stand
tall waiting for that call to arms.
Where enemies threaten our wellbeing
these brave hearts rise to the occasion
with absolute dedication. For our
soldiers are strong and highly
skilled as the act of war is
very real. To tear down
and rebuild, broken
hearts will heal,
soldiers will die,
and soldiers will
rise and for
soldiers many
will cry.

July 6, 2015

MICHAEL WAYNE BRYANT

The Man Behind The Mirror

I had rather been born blind
into a world where I couldn't
see, because I hate the man
behind the mirror
Known as me. With
a heart full of strife for
a fool and a soul dark like the
greatest depths of the ocean,
empty and hopeless. My
definition of beauty
was corrupted by the impurities
of my mind hidden deep
inside, but in time these
atrocities disciplined
me with a new sense
of direction. Now
that man behind the
mirror has a Brand
New Reflection.

September 3, 2007

Life Amazing

Here we go with the ego
or maybe it's the pride that
arise from inside in either
case a poor choice of taste
life is never a waste, divided
we stand, separated by
beliefs and land, life is
amazing, but humanity don't
understand as twisted
thoughts chop off the hand
of morality leaving love stranded
causes fatalities, mental
riptides sweep aside the
ability to think rationally and
in time your capacity to function
sinks dramatically, you become
the focus of you and when
that happens there's no limit
to what you might do, yet
even in the darkness of our ignorance,
life is amazing and forever
more magnificent.

November 20, 2015

Sam I Am

Sam I am
Never gave a damn,
All he knew was the streets
And that's all he'll ever be. See,
he had a life full of grief, losing
his parents at the age of three and
may they both rest in peace.
He was sent to New York City to live
with his uncle Cee, but that wasn't
a gain just a shame to live in
poverty. From that day forth, Sam
I am never looked back and at
the age of ten he started selling
crack. At the age of seventeen,
what was a dream turned to
reality as he lived a life
filled with luxuries. By
the age of twenty he was
Known by many with no
remorse or pity his
attitude was quite
gritty, but that's how
it is living in the
city.

March 2, 2012

Prison Blues

How can you deliver me
if you can't see all the misery
poured on me or the overflowing
of prisons with the forgotten ones,
fathers, brothers, uncles, and
sons, it's a test of true sincerity,
but without loyalty becomes a
bittersweet rivalry between
family or friends, where time don't
only heal wounds, but dry up
relationships like cocoons of dried
bones called fossils a colossal
of devastation so where's the
motivation, no communication
becomes feelings of hatred, I tried to
explain it, but your comprehension could
not sustain it, so your thoughts became
tainted, separated by miles of
dirt and pavement, years turn into
decades that constantly chip away
family ties as loved ones begin to die,
funerals multiply, no more tears you
can't even cry.

October 4, 2015

Irony

You see it
in the movies
and read about
it in books, but
you never become worried,
until it becomes your reality.
Then it stabs you in the back, sending
chills down your spine as it
manifest within the mind.
For its only purpose is when
something strange can't be
explained and that alone
can play tricks on the
brain, eventually
driving you
insane.

March 3, 2012

True Fact

Her presence in God's
 creation was a blessing
  to man to be fruitful
   and multiple in the land.
Her elegance is irrelevant,
 but her essence goes without
  question in hand.
To have and to hold her
 is truly a gift, otherwise
  man could have never made it
with a lifeline connected
 to her baby, she remains stable
  To endure nine months
   of labor and
to show my appreciation this
 poem was written about a
  woman's dedication.

January 30, 2007

Where's The Love

Obviously,
people make life hard, when it's supposed to
be easy. Complexity, complexity and more
complexity. Where is the simplicity in
all of this misery with hidden agendas
surrounded by pretenders.
Common enemies, envy and jealousy
causing robberies and murder in the
first degree. Why, so much violence, it's
no mystery take a hard look at history.
What a tragedy that's gradually
bringing humanity down like gravity,
hear that sound. "You make my love
come down," but where's the love now?
Exhaustion fills the hearts of most,
killing dreams and hopes from the
top of mountain slopes to your inner
most.
So, let your determination ignite like
dynamite causing a chain reaction
around the world to unite despite
your color, it's to help each other one soul
to another.
Shattering all thoughts of evil like
glass, slow down objects in the mirror
move too fast, lose touch with reality
and you won't last.

September 15, 2014

When I Die

Let there be a
celebration of my cremation
or a burial of my flesh
and bones
followed by a line
of mourners,
but Jesus warned us,
so cry not
for the plot of the story
is not to worry,
the soul don't cease
to exist with the last breath,
that's only a physical death,
for my essence was
never in question
sealed with God's blessings.
As the spiritual me
ascends,
my memories I
leave in your presence,
'cause I made it to heaven.

August 1, 2015

Fear The Darkness

It's sneaky when it's crawling,
creepy when it's stalking and
  only come out when the sun starts
    falling.
      Then it hovers behind you like a
        cloud, reaching out as you try to
          scream, but your voice becomes
          silent like a bad dream.
            You shake and shiver, paralyzed
            in fear for noise it doesn't
              make, but you know that it's
              near and just before the
              darkness over-take,
              click,
                who turn on the lights
                or who's afraid of
                the night.

                    March 5, 2010

My Analysis

Chapter after chapter
I been writing in this book called life,
never with a pen, words out of
sight, mentally handwritten
never typed, experiences—some
wrong, some right, choices and
consequences turn into
verbal and physical responses,
motivated by the character
I play in this movie I live every day
and getting up in age makes me
afraid that I might be turning
my last page, but the fact
is no matter what happens after
the flick of the wrist, know this,
life is full of bliss like a sweet
dish of a long goodnight kiss,
a memoir of memories that I
will never forget.

September 11, 2015

Spring Again!

It's winter end, spring again, but only
for a short phase of ninety days then
back again cause it's spring again.
Bright colors, clear skies and dark
shades to cover the eyes. Jackets and
long sleeves no longer needed,
short sleeves and shorts helps
the body from becoming over
heated. Rain feeds the greenery,
changing the whole scenery
as the temperature rise
warm air will blow causing
pollen to float as the
mold and fungus will
grow. When the heat looms,
watch nature bloom. Birds will
sing and the leaves will turn green.
Insects will climb from their holes and
animals will crawl from their burrows.
Eggs will hatch and cocoons will burst,
stand back mother nature at work!

November 20, 2014

Dazed and Confused

Dazed by the phase
          of ordinary days,
trapped and barricaded
          in our minds,
surrounded by land mines
          of space and time
while awaiting a solution
          to the chaos and
pollution, parallel dimensions
          radiate tension
Einstein and his brilliant
          invention, a divine
intervention, but is it
          too little too late
for something so small
          so great, radioactive
and waiting for something
          to happen, but too
confused to lose, yet
          so nice and smooth
like a genuine chess move.

          July 7, 2015

The Inner Self Apocalypse

Its pure power in transforming,
 the sound of killer bees swarming,
   Red lights flashing – warning!
You can't contain it,
 it's insane.
    This thing they call pain
      set fire to your veins like cocaine.
        Have you calling names and
          doing crazy things.
That relentless beast
 that feeds on agony,
   causing nothing but havoc.
What's tragic is it's
 really you in reality, no technicality.
    Trained in the field,
      death valley or hamburger hill
        and breathless as you may feel
          Thank God it's not real.

November 30, 2014

Me and the Cat in the Tree

Yes, it's just an ordinary tree, but
it is special to me, because unlike
people this tree listens wholeheartedly.
Whether sunshine, rain, sleet, or
snow, I come by daily to say hello,
but on this particular day there
was a difference in the energy flow.
At first, I thought something was
missing, then my eyes caught the new
addition, sitting on a branch
dressed in black fur with green eyes
and a loud purr. It stood its ground
and so did I as we locked eye to eye.
Movement on either end and a war
would begin. I wasn't afraid, but this
cat was strangely brave. I screamed
and yelled, but it wouldn't be chased
away and his eyes looked as if to
say, I'm here to stay. I became exhausted
and took a set beneath the tree, then
closed my eyes for a second and guess
who was sitting next to me. Mr. Friendly,
the cat from the tree as I quickly
realized this cat was a lot like me,
lonely. So, I just let things be and
in time we became a family, me and
the cat in the tree.

September 17, 2016

The Butterfly Effect

I can't live in the past,
it's already gone. I can live for the
moment, but even that won't last long.
I can only hope that my life
will serve a purpose, because right now
I'm feeling quite worthless.
It's damned if you do and
damned if you don't, damned if you will
and damned if you won't.
Literally I'm dying within,
but figuratively I just want to live.
I'm in a place filled with shadows,
each one fighting its own battle.
A lone soldier within the
mind, ducking and dodging trying
to stay alive, but all frivolous
because in the end you still die. So
don't ask why, because what's done is
done just make peace with
yourself until that day come.

November 2, 2014

I See You

I see you
  trying to hide, but
    the eyes you can't disguise.
I see you
  Watching me watch you
    as if you don't know why
      like the sun watching the
        moon in the sky.
I see you
  watching every moment
    of life 'cause your essence
      is love with a smile of delight.
I see you
  through all the flesh and bones
    and beyond the mind
      you're all holy and divine.
I see you
  as I see myself, because
    the truth is there is no
      one else.

February 13, 2017

Yesterday, Today and Tomorrow

Yesterday-
　is the past,
　　so that's where I let it be.
　　　why some of us hang on to it,
　　　　beats the hell out of me.
Today-
　is a new beginning
　　and for the moment we
　　　are all winning. Where desires
　　　　and secrets of the heart is
　　　　　constantly unfolding makes it
　　　　　　golden.
Tomorrow-
　is not here yet, so we live with NO
　　regret. So weep not, because Yesterday
　　　is gone, today is constantly fleeting
　　　　and to worry about tomorrow
　　　　　is self-defeating.

March 5, 2015

My Window

From my window
I can see nature unfold
and seasons change from hot to cold,
while clouds roll by like crimson tides
yielding to the sun in the sky, watching
her rays bathe the shrubs and
trees with energy raising the
dead to a beautiful greenery,
a picture-perfect scenery to
see life in motion, waking
up to the early morning
dew drops or to the
loud commotion of
children waiting
at the bus stop, the barking of dogs or
a cat's meow, birds singing in harmony
all bringing back some childhood
memories with the pouring of rain sending dirt down the
drains as the wind blows
rustling the dead leaves
all from my window.

February 21, 2017

Dilemma

Every Friday night
the good met at Christine's,
A routine since they were teens.
 A record unmatched
   by any other guest and
      their loyalty to one another
         was more than just a journey,
            but a quest.
Love and compassion
was always first giving them
time to flirt. Then came in
discipline, patience and kindness,
they always had great timing. The
other two being generosity and
consideration was always late, but
that's another debate.
Nevertheless they were all there
 with much laughter, joy and peace
   in the air. Thery had much to be thankful
      for as they celebrated and hit
         the dance floor.
The music was pumping
and the crowd was jumping.
Then suddenly the
music stopped and a glass
dropped.
Just then, the double doors
 flew open and everything seemed
   to be in slow motion with a small
      guest of wind as the seven deadly
         sins came walking in.
All the guests quickly dispersed

in knowing things were headed
for the worst. Evil calmly took
up seats at a nearby table and
ordered plates of steaks
with baked potatoes.
The dance floor was completely
 empty and the guest tables were
    clear as the good stood near. There
       wasn't a sound and if you listened
          hard enough you could hear sweat
             hitting the ground.
Remember the tree of good
and evil in the Bible that's the
key, these two have a long
fought history. A rivalry passed
on since the beginning of time
for the total control of the Soul,
body and mind.
A battle of equal force
 with God being the primary
    source. Meanwhile, the good
       returned to their seats not to eat
          or retreat, but to keep an eye on
             their adversaries.
Evil was becoming anxious
and losing their patience, but
hate told them to wait. The tension
had reached its peak for each of them
possessed a highly skilled technique
that was deadly and unique.
Love decided to move first
 and gave a nod to consideration,
    who then jumped up and did a flip
       off the table sending him airborne
          while throwing stars that cut the

electrical cable.
The only light that loomed
was from the moon that reflected
off a spoon letting hate know patience
was making his move as the
blade of his sword gave him a
close shave. Just millimeters closer
and his head would have been off his
shoulders.
Then greed stepped out of
 the shadows, a tenth degree
    Black belt in karate. Who then
       approached discipline, a Zen
          master who specialized in
             self-defense.
The battle began with a roundhouse
kick from greed to the head of
discipline, who caught it with the back
of his wrist and then gave it a sharp
twist, shattering the bone like a
piece of glass sending bone fragments
through the air.
Greed screamed in agony
 as he fell to the floor begging for his life
    as discipline grabbed him by the
       neck and choked out his air until
          nothing was left causing
             his death.
Seconds later a knife was thrown
out of the dark that pierced
discipline through the heart. It
became an all out war in the middle
of the dance floor.
The steel on steel sparks
 lit up the dark, showing

*the sharpness of their blades, which
sliced through each other in every
which way. The gushing of blood
stained the walls and covered
the floor in red, in just a matter
of minutes they were all dead.*
Except one,
who remained standing in the blood-
soaked room, reminder us all of the
inner war we must all go through.
Whether or not love conquers all
is another brawl, but for now it's the
end until a new dilemma within
self rises up again.

December 5, 2014

Shake
It
Off

Shake
it
off
like
a
champion,
growling
like
a
panther,
sing a song like an
anthem,
scratching
and clawing
your way
back
bouncing
like a ball
telling life
to take
that!

February 28, 2017

Else-Where

I'm in love
with that fire that
consumes your soul, but
your eyes tell of another story
yet to be told. I love you with
all of my heart and not
just usually, but even when you
sometime act so foolishly. So I ask
myself, do you feel the same or
are you playing some kind of
mental game. Maybe I need to look
else-where, so when you look up and
I'm no longer there. It wasn't
magic, I didn't just
disappear into thin air.
You didn't care, so
I went else-where.

December 6, 2014

A Lifetime

Quick as it comes
quick as it leaves
destiny
is the tree that
bore the seeds
and
life is the soil
that nurtures our
needs, but
death is the gardener
who
plucks the weeds.

May 18, 2018

If Only For A Moment

I cling to it
with the greatest of love,
but it always fly away like
a dove. So radical
in its approach as it ascends
like smoke, springing up like grass
just to be ripped from my
grasp. I know that I will
never own it, but I solicit to the
moment. Small like the grains of
sand that slips through the hands.
If only for a second, never
regretting its touch like passion.
Something I love so very
much, but never seems to be enough.
Yearning like a spark in the
dark to become a flame, it's a shame
to think that I could ever change
anything. For the moment is not the
prisoner of time nor time the
prisoner of the moment.

April 4, 2015

The Scale of Justice

Even in the midst
of all this madness there
is a balance called
happiness
that heals the hearts of those
filled with sadness,
where hate rules
hearts of fools that
reign, but only for a
short period of time before
love retakes its claim.

June 5, 2017

Problems

Problems, Problems and
Problems is there no end to this synonym
of a pendulum that's slowly killing
them with each swing bringing
with it degrees of misery
and pain. So, who is the
blame, because I've been wrecking my
brain like a
ball and chain,
the results are always
the same. Therefore,
the one who complains is
probably the one to
blame.

March 25, 2015

One Extraordinary Day

If rated,
 it would earn
  one hundred percent.
   A day that seems like
    heaven sent, perfect in
     every sense as if it was
      meant to be just for me, tailor
       made from the finest of fabrics
        a moment in time so fantastic
        absent the chaos and tragic
        events that usually plague
       the present with prayers
      of repent, but not today,
     for today is one of those
    extraordinary days, but
   come tomorrow, I must
  turn the page watching
today fade away,
causing tears to fall
from my eyes as I
can only wave to it
goodbye.

August 24, 2015

The Recipe For Poetry

All recipes call
for something, but
not too much just a
little of a poet's touch.
The manuscript is real, something
you can feel. Take a taste, yet be
careful not to waste and watch the ink
liquidate the lines that confine this paper.
The more ingredients, the greater the flavor
to savor. My cliché say long and sleek
is clever, but short and sweet just sounds
better. Giving you something strange a
magical thing like musical instruments
being played without the strings made
of nightmares and sweet dreams.
I hope you enjoyed this
entrée of edible and
incredible words, so
magnificent not even
a remnant was
imminent.

April 6, 2015

I Trusted You

I trusted you with
my heart, but you let me
mown. A dream turned
into a nightmare, life
upside down, struck
by a poisonous dart of
your vicious intentions, I'd
rather be eaten whole by
a shark and my death never
mentioned. You ravaged my soul
with lies leaving me covered
with flies, now look into my eyes
I have already died, see what you
done, death without a gun, you
insidious heifer, the work of a
lethal injection, a cannabis of
a woman that caused me to stumble.
Even now I don't wonder as my soul
roars like a lion in the jungle, but now
humbled, I just play the hand I was
dealt without anybody knowing
that her murder is what I truly felt.

September 3, 2015

This Old House

I bought a house
 with a history,
Seventy-five years old
 that's three quarters
of a century. One house
 in the middle of nowhere
is a mystery, but without
 the nosey neighbors
is a luxury.
 The first night was scary
with all the strange and eerie
 sounds, but it is said
that old houses have a spooky
 way of settling down.
Sounds crazy, but it's true
 for there is a lot of work I
have to do, like eradicating
 all the roaches, rats and
bats in the attic.
 Then I have to insulate
the walls, because every time
 the wind blows it feels like
an open window. Water-proof
 the roof to stop the
leaks that swell the floor
 boards causing them
to squeak. Cut the tree
 limbs that scrape against
the window pane every time
 it rains and all the same
don't forget about the leaky
 faucets drop after drop

non-stop or what about the
 lights that blink every time
the phone rings. Kind of makes
 you think of a haunted house,
but if I didn't know better,
 I might have moved out.

April 11, 2015

Taking Nothing for Granted

I live with no regrets
every second is precious
as I make the best of it,
never spilling or wasting it,
slow and steady never chasing it.
My idea of life isn't
crooked or slanted,
nothing is taken for granted.
So, I tell you every day in every way
that I love you just in case I suddenly
pass away, leaving no doubt about
what came out of my mouth,
because there's nothing else I need
to say, every opportunity is
utilized, solid in thought
crystalized, every breath
realized until this story
called life is finalized.

September 6, 2015

More Than Flesh and Bones

Genetics and cold fusion,
echoes of physics already
proven.
Energy, the key to heat and
the core of the human anatomy
as with every heartbeat that
causes the blood to flow from the
head down to the toe, a
cycle with no end until
you're deceased. The brain
is like a puppet master
controlling everything without
strings, from A to Z the entire
chemistry in how we function
in this vast galaxy. Made not just
of flesh and bones, but of
a soul that sits on its throne within
the heart as it keeps us breathing, but
for what reason. A spiritual journey
saint or heathen or just a sparkle
in God's eye, so why ask why,
just live then die.

April 9, 2015

Rainbows

With their many
colors,
blue,
red,
and yellow,
starting in one place
and
ending in another
that
bends like a piece of
rubber
to formulate a giant
archway,
some large and some
small
then suddenly it dissolves,
but
just to have seen it
was a blessing in all.

March 2, 2012

The Vow

It's a marriage
ceremony in
the joining of two people,
the greatest of all sequels.
Partners and lovers
joined hand in hand for better
or worst, rich or poor or until
life is no more,
what do you think the rings
are for,
symbolizing where love adore
forever more. A sacred
ritual uniting one plus one
equal one, holy in all
scriptures and should
never be
undone.

April 23, 2015

Masquerade

One face with many expressions raises
a series of questions, a mirror reflection
of motions that can change in a blink
of a moment, looks to be genuine, but
personified into a lie too hard to
deny no matter how much we try,
so many cover their face with
masks to meet the task at hand,
but fake hearts are quickly
exposed that crumble like sand,
faces that never remain the
same in a game of who is
who is insane, but this is
true in all that we do,
constantly putting on faces
of deception don't always
fall through and sometimes
people will see the real
you.

September 11, 2015

Lies

Ocean tides
constantly flow in and out,
so do the lies that come out
of our mouth. Every lie has a
storyline with a theme and as
strange as it may be, it
becomes enticing with a little
reality busting from the seams.
There are varieties of
reasons why people lie, but
the truth is none can be justified,.
Lies exist endlessly and
multiply tremendously. It is a
part of us more so than the
truth, look around at the
preponderance of proof. If
this is true, then I guess
all that we think we know
could be a lie too.

May 2, 2015

The Flim-Flam

It's tragic how I run game,
but you're a willing participant
so who's to blame.
When I flip a card or roll
the dice many are enticed,
but that's the glitz and the
glamour of the fast life.
Money comes slowly, but
leaves quickly, my hands
move too swiftly leaving your
pockets empty, a game of
finesse, Buddha bless, not
checkers or chess, I make
a living doing this, money
hand over fist, skills of
a perfectionist, now pay up
you owe me twenty for just
reading this.

August 4, 2015

Just A Dream

You are the perfect
representation of my imagination.
for the eyes don't lie as I realized
that I missed my calling, because
my lips upon yours is where they
should be falling. Undressing you
with my eyes, I become blinded
by the beauty of your hips and
thighs in your nakedness.
Reaching out to find the landing
of my hands upon your breast.
Which I did not hesitate
to suck, your twin mountain
crest, causing saliva to trickle
down to your heaveness saturated
by your natural moistness. Gracefully
penetrating you with my penis and
exploded like a rocket taking off for
Venus just to wake up and realize I
was dreaming.

May 13, 2015

I Wonder

I always wanted to see
what others seen in me, because
 what I see is not how things
 really be,
making the idea of myself
 a twisted reality
that I don't quite understand,
 because if I did, I would
know that I am much more
 than just a man, but
    more like a grain of sand
on the beach of God's great
 plan that seems so
insignificant in such a vast
 universe, makes me think to
myself, what did God create
    first?

September 12, 2015

Racist

They plague the earth like leaves on trees, a mental disease that's ruthless as a psychopath with no sympathy. Twisted individuals hiding behind tinted glasses like spies in a movie classic. They hate, because they just do and don't need a reason to kill me or you. These are the people who represent the ugly face of racism and by their nature feel superior over your existence. As sick as it may sound this is the reality of what's being spread around. A poisonous mindset that is a risk to all who exist.

May 9, 2015

Faces

Can't put a name
 to all the faces,
  but I love them all
   like exotic
    places.
Never been a racist,
 I see God in them
  no way an atheist.
   Look at what God created,
    so holy and sacred, all
     equal without discrimination,
      so, nobody owes anybody an
       explanation.

February 7, 2016

Serene

I write
mental pictures
called stanzas like
Michaelangelo painted
on canvases, then barricaded
your thoughts in emotions and
put your ability to think in Hypnosis.
Just before switching gears, causing
you to slip into a state of
unconsciousness
leaving your
body
      stranded without prognosis
        This is the legacy of my pedigree
      covered by a canopy of words.
     However described, you will
    awaken feeling cool, calm
   and energized not realizing
you just been mentally
serenaded by a great
narrator.

May 15, 2015

Diversity

Change
    is
        inevitable,
              beautiful
                    and incredible.

The quest of
    evolution
      at its best,
    perfectly manifested
        and
    hand crafted
        by the
            master Himself,
where the unlimited
    supply to meet the
        demands of the
            universe
                comes
                    first.

February 6, 2016

Revenge

They say revenge is best
served cold, but this
one was burning hot. Where
you become a victim of an
unsolved murder plot.
No evidence on who done it
or how they got away with
it, because Karma don't
forget and forgiveness wasn't
in the manuscript. So,
it must be true, be careful
in what you say or do,
because this could happen
to you.

May 9, 2015

What's the Value of Life?

This ain't Wall Street.
Life isn't a commodity
 trying to make a profit.
  Interest rates keep dropping,
   Phantom of the Opera,
    people disappearing,
     black market
      everyone's a target.
So, what's the value of life?
 Afraid and scattering like mice,
  I guess human trafficking is
   alright 'cause no one willing
    to fight and being sold
     for a price, then ask
      yourself what's the
       value of life?
Where murder is more common
 than a cold and gold is
  appreciated more than the
   human soul, if life exists
    death will unfold, hearts
     of stone don't sympathize.
Stocks and bonds
 on the rise, the truth
  is yet to be realized,
   while the poor seek a slice, but
    what's the value of life?
Reality ignites like dynamite
 camouflaged killers roam the night
  seeking the lives of those who've
   seen the light, dignity and
    prestige don't exist and

tyrants rule the lands
  with an iron fist.
So, I ask you this, what is the value
 of life?

November 25, 2015

Ghost Writer

My name will remain unacclaim,
because I don't write just
to entertain.
It's the words that deserve
your attention, so powerful
and relentless.
Nevertheless, I am
one of the best in manifesting words
into sentences, relishing the
mental with food to digest
is so simple. It's
elementary, so take notes
on the documentary of the
century and the last
of my epitome.

May 29, 2015

To Be or Not to Be

If to be
 is just to exist
  that is ignorance,
   for the greatest of all
    wealth is the awakening
     of self,
      because
       the reality
        is spirituality
         and that's deliverance.

February 13, 2016

Beat The Drum

When you feel like
           your life is done,
                    Beat the drum.
All anger and frustration flow free,
           Trust me I know,
                    Beat the drum.
The impact of your hands beating down
           on the canvas drums causes
             a vibration that creates
              a stupendous sensation,
                  Beat the drum.
When you're saddened by the woes of life
           and overtaken by the
             strife, don't give up just
              fight, Beat the drum,
                Beat the drum,
                Beat the drum,
Until your hands get tired or your
           life expires, because your
            heart still beats with
             the same desires of the
              ancient past that gave
               them the power of
                endurance to outlast.
So get up, dust yourself off
           and don't take life so
            seriously, but have some
             fun like starting now,
                 Beat the drum.

                              June 11, 2015

Drama Is

Drama is
being suspended in time with
  too much excitement twirling
    through the mind.
Drama is
our physical vibrations running
  on high, now picture life without
    this sad reality.
Drama is
the groom or bride in a marriage
  and our love for it is like a baby in
    a carriage.
Drama is
mental intoxication with sober
  complications that leaves us trembling
    from all the adrenaline.
Drama is
turning another page in the book of
  escapades, the how we die, the how
    we live, and how we destroy then
      rebuild, all for the thrill.
Drama is
blaming suspense as our cause of intent,
  because we won't live without it, knowing
    its damage is permanent.

March 20, 2016

Spontaneous

Hot I'm not,
but determine,
chest burning from sips of bourbon.
Car swerving out of control
and another dead body lie cold on
the road, as crows peck away on
the carcass, weak stomach
feeling nauseous.
Panic and become
hysterical, mindset
no longer lyrical.
Interest become miserable
and overwhelmed by the negative,
frustration leads to exaggeration
can't focus no concentration.
Patience is hard to come by
no understanding for senseless
drive-bys. Situation powerless
events happen continuous
that makes life so spontaneous!

June 16, 2015

Here Today, Gone Tomorrow

Just yesterday,
  I was a baby crying
    and now today I'm just
      an old man dying.

I sometimes wonder,
  where did all the years go.
    Now, I just sit and stare
      out of the window, sometime
        I even cry without asking
      why or without a care.

Just happy to see the closing
  of another year go so gently
    and silently into the
      atmosphere.

June 28, 2015

True Friends

I say thank you
 to all of those who stood by me
  in my times of trouble, your support
   was nothing short of love as
    my enemies just pushed and shoved,
Trying to make me fall,
 but thanks to your aid, I conquered
  it all.
Now I know to appreciate
 and recognize true friends and
  will stick with them through
   thick or thin, for true friends
stand by each other until
 the end,
the rest just crumble
 and blow away in the wind.

July 14, 2007

MICHAEL WAYNE BRYANT

The Scenario

Picture this, a screen play too fast for the NASCAR speedway. Nickels and dimes, old religious scrolls and shrines, twelve in all when combined, the zodiac signs. Insolent behavior, Jesus the savior, God the creator, tales and fables. Eminent danger, border patrol or Texas ranger. Foreign delinquent coming more frequent, animal kingdom headed for extinction. All is relevant, be benevolent, get belligerent and show ignorance. While scholars search history for ancient lies and conspiracies, hypocrisy and military secrecy a government agency. Nuclear explosion, political slogans, despite life and its obstacles to know God is not impossible. The opposite of logical, become angry and hostile. From the physical to the spiritual, it's all in scenario. Where dreams become schemes of no reality, angels and demons fight for principalities. Now, flatter me with your jittery gestures and dissertation of explanations on life. What's wrong or right, the shoulds and should not as if I forgot.

July 3, 2015

Throw Away People

The value of life
doesn't come with a price,
people are put through hellish conditions
just for spite, the poor being the
sacrifice, money is cash,
the less fortunate being trash,
no regards for creation
throwing away people like raw
sanitation, plantations
of slums and ghettos
war without medals,
laughing and grinning
at their stupidity, openly
and without pity, donating
to a few charities is your
fight for humanity, but
being rich isn't the problem,
it's your insanity.

September 10, 2015

My Sanctuary

My sanctuary
is sacred and lies
within my own
reality.
My sanctuary
is raining down in
love and compassion,
totally relaxing
and everlasting.
My sanctuary
is a place of complete
bliss and harmonious,
but many don't
believe in it.
It may sound crazy,
but my sanctuary
is amazing and
in every heart
there is a safe
haven.

June 30, 2015

Pure Adrenaline

With every breath my breathing becomes
more erratic, lungs expand like a
rubber band sporadic, creating
energy called static, more
oxygen I got to have, sweat
forms on my brow leaving
puddles at my feet, body
heat raising the humidity.
Muscles become tense
and rigid, skin
moist and glistening.
Tendons and
ligaments
twitching
from
the quickness
of my agility,
from density to the
intensity of my stamina
is phenomenal in its ability
to endure more, extreme stress on the core
with an ounce more of pure adrenaline.
Just a letter to my competitors, take
heed from the editor.

September 15, 2015

Bonafide

It was written by the dignified
washed in holy water
and certified.
Many died, but only one
was crucified.
Never realizing the
words spoken, the masses
lost focus. Pages were
torn from its book over the
ages by demonic hands of
hatred. Only scattered paper
of human remains exist,
like a sweet kiss of Authenticity
and one hundred percent of
simplicity. Resurrected
because it never died,
Bonafide.

July 19, 2015

Tempo

I like my tempo smooth,
 a trendy groove with a flow
   that won't let go.
A pedal to the metal type
 of half note that begins
   with a violin intro to a single
     piano key note followed by
       my lead, the maestro.
Signaling for the symphony in whole
 while my hands compose whole
   notes into sound, swirling
     melodies lifting you off the
       ground, flipping and turning
         you around just before gently
           sitting you back down.
But it's not over yet, because you're
 about to get the eighth to the
   sixteenth note, the gold crown
     of music that's guaranteed to
       have you standing in ovation
         and elation in a dramatic
           fashion, because you just
             witnessed another classic.

September 12, 2015

Progress

Every little step
is a plus
that lives within all of us,
add it up and
call it calculus.
Where mindfulness
is relentless as physical
fitness is in our
pursuit of happiness.
For the
reasonable and emotional
is like
checks and balances
being subjected
to selfishness with no awareness
spells thoughtlessness,
but nevertheless
it's progress
and nothing less.

July 26, 2015

Exclusive

This is for the third-eye minded
not the spiritually blinded
and very rarely will you ever
find it though
hidden deep within your
own confinements.
Seek not, want not, essence
the size of a dot, light getting dim,
outcome looking grim.
Nevertheless, it's all a quest
of the shrine of the inner self,
a token of the unspoken hidden
wealth, where few are chosen,
ancient dialects remain frozen.
Mountains on high one must
climb through the slopes of
ignorance just to find thyself
behind the mind, one throne,
one creator all alone with the
whole truth written in stone.

September 7, 2015

The Struggle

The trouble with life
is the struggle of the fight
you never win, over, over and
over again.

    It's like being violently torn
apart by demonic hands in the
dark, no Noah's ark only the
high seas of miseries attacking
you spiritually.

    You scream out in hopes of
amnesty, but your voice echoes
in the valley of duality, for
travesty creates reality that
brings about the finale.

July 21, 2015

Dear America

What I'm about
to say applies to everyone this very day.
Some will hate it
and others will debate it, no
matter what it can't be erased and
must be faced. For a country that is
so great, its history is filled with
much misery especially slavery and
even though it's been many moons
ago, I can still feel every blow.
I suffer as if
I was there, I can taste
it in the air, it's everywhere.
I can see the unspeakable methods
used to abuse and kill my
ancestors with and it is
something I can never forget.
More black men, women, and
children died in it than any
war. None of them received
a medal of honor for their
bravery, all they
got was a bullet and a grave
with a handmade headstone out of
wood. A wooden cross, tossed
and looted from strong winds,
the ultimate price for
anyone to pay for the color
of their skin. Yet this
country wants to bury it
instead of acknowledging it,
and even though things have changed

with time, it's still fresh
in many minds. Slavery is
like a forbidden word never to be
spoken like a worthless token
a wound that still lies open. So
in order for it to heal this country
must break the seal of silence
and speak on this unforgettable
violence.
Slavery was more than just an
acquisition, but a condition that
has placed us in our present position.
Even when slavery ended a new
form of racism was implemented.
The chains were taken off of us
physically and placed on us mentally.
They said we were free,
but that would never be for if
that was true then why did we
have to go through so many trials
and tribulations just to be a part
of this nation. We helped this
nation become great, we fought
and died in wars right beside
you and my skin didn't matter then.
The fight wasn't with me
it was for your freedom,
justice and equality. No matter
how many of us die or how
hard we try, we will never
be seen as an equal in your
society. Sometimes I wonder do
you really understand the
ramifications of how slavery
traumatized us mentally.

Making jealousy and envy our enemy,
because of your hate a stake
was driven between us. Where there
was once trust is now disgust.
You made us believe that the
color of our skin was a sin
and with the help of time
it spread to our minds.
So, how can we help one another
if we hate one another, which
means we don't love one another
makes it easy to kill one another,
so there is no way we can heal
one another. An explanation
is not needed, but an apology
would be well-greeted if it's from
the bottom of your heart, then
a true healing process can
start. It's not a
matter of who done what or
looking for someone to blame.
This problem must be resolved
so this country can continue to
evolve.

January 22, 2013

The Tree of Life

It was the thought
that brought about the seed.
Which was planted in the
dirt of eternity and watered
in lore that grew into a great
tree of prestige.
Its branches produced
the fruitage of life
with delight, but the leaves
of the ego created a world
of strife with no sympathy.
Now, like a common cold
every soul is faced with
this common enemy.

July 12, 2015

Rain

(1) I love the rain
in all its forms,
a mist, drizzle,
or thunderstorm.

(2) When it rains
I never complain
because to me it's all
the same, Mother Nature
doing her work in purifying
the earth and washing away
the dirt.

(3) Thunderstorms get my
attention real quick,
especially when the lightning
hit and that thunder seems
to never quit.

(4) Quite charming and alarming,
but calmness does come once the
downpour is done.

(5) The drizzle is like a chisel
banging away, with a constant
flow of rain that lasts all day,
and let's not forget about the
mist, so cool and crisp
that floats in the air
like vapors in the month
of April.

(6) Whether heavy or light,

day or night, the rain
is always cold. That
seems to penetrate my
flesh down to my naked soul.

(7) The sound of rain
    hitting metal sings a
    melody that soothes me
    internally, something like
    the Holy Ghost moving me
    spiritually.

(8) But it's the enigma within
    that triggers me mentally
    to be in harmony while
    constantly counting the drops,
    but I often fall asleep
    before the rain stops.

December 8, 2014

Problematic

Assume the position
from the streets to prisons.
Reckless citizen, NO hope
for transition, mind over-haul
demolition.
Argumentative,
Never relentless, NO
comment, actions
speak louder than
words, no logic.
Heart demented
like a chemist
cemented in hate,
hell bent on actions
that will seal your
fate.

September 13, 2015

Planet Earth

The sky, the land, and the sea for as far
as I can see, oh what beauty you hold
century after century as you surround
yourself in a cluster of stars and plants
like a single rose in the garden of
heaven. The universe is your mother
and you are her child, so tender
and mild. The sun rays bathe
you in heat creating energy
to give you a heartbeat.
You rotate on your axle
with joy like a baby
with a toy, so consumed
with excitement and
always at peace. Your
clouds liquidate the land
with water causing the trees
and plants to grow taller. You
have mountain tops covered in snow,
showing the world how high you can
go. You bore flowers of all sorts and colors,
your vegetables and fruits are firm
and sweet that provides for all
of humanity, so thank you!

May 14, 2007

Zenith

Everyday,
   we face the threat of regrets,
     a spiritual famine of mental
      challenges that needs to be
      balanced.

      Where deluded morals turn
     into elusive plays hidden in
     the decoys of illusion. OH, what
     tangle web we weave, nothing but
     confusion. For enough is enough to
the point of no return and at the
crossroad of the soul is where life will
yearn.

       July 30, 2015

Just A Drop

I'm just a drop of water
don't pay me any mind,
I fall from the sky all of the
time, there are millions of
me within a cloud, as I float
about I may just stop and
let it all out saving the land
from a severe drought, a
source of life to the mouth and
when consumed I become
seventy percent of your resident
as well as the planet, I
liquidate and regenerate all
life, without me your
reality would be nothing more
than cosmic dust in this
galaxy.

September 3, 2015

I Just Cry About It

I have tried to hold it in,
 but it just keep coming back
  time and time again.
   Those emotions of mine
    causes nothing, but tears of
     commotion in my mind.
      I deny not in what I see,
       for the pain and suffering
        of this world really affects
         me, so I just cry about it,
          yeah I just cry about it.

I turn my head in regret,
 but those prickly hairs on my
  neck won't let me forget. We
   could talk about this forever,
    but still would never ever no
     matter how clever we may be,
      understand the God in humanity.
       So just continue to fight the good
        fight until- you die, so just
         cry about it,
          yeah I just cry about it
           and that's no lie.

July 26, 2015

Flick of the Switch

From zero to sixty is clockable, but from
curious to insidious is unstoppable,
one on the brink of being diabolical,
confrontation methodical, yet
practical for the irrational,
but the mentally deranged
is undetectable, treatable
if foreseeable, nothing
short of unpredictable
no tell-tale signs
only victims left
behind, questions
of who, what
or why
is
established
in a situation where
people die is tragic, but
fortunately for society this
is a thin portfolio of a seldomly
seen scenario.

September 7, 2015

Imagine This

*If the mind stop,
you think not and reality
becomes a blank spot. Kinks
in the links of creativity, no
stimulation causes dead
motivation, no exaggeration
or focus without imagination
life is hopeless.*

September 16, 2015

MICHAEL WAYNE BRYANT

The Cabin in the Woods

The candlelight flickers
as small drops of water trickle
from the holes in the ceiling as
shadows form on the wall
from the glow, the breeze from the
cracks feels like an open window,
wood in the fireplace burns low,
ground covered in feet of snow,
stranded and nowhere else to go,
water partially frozen and
barely flowing, cabinets full
of miscellaneous, but nothing
edible or life sustaining, the
accumulation of dust means
years without a human touch,
sun rays seep through the holes in
the sack cloth that hangs from
the sill and fills the room
with the odor of mildew, shuffling
to an old rocking chair that sat
in the corner gave me some peace,
rocking myself to sleep to suddenly
being woken by someone's hand on
my shoulder.

September 11, 2015

Reminiscence

A moment in time
being held at the present,
stories and secrets once
lost in the desert of the mind.
Seek and you shall find, knock
and watch it turn back the hands
on a clock, consciousness clear and
solid as a rock, déjà vu all over again,
but consequently this is just
reminiscence something like pretending,
because every story has an
ending.

September 14, 2015

Stripped

Bare essentials
are the building blocks
for elementals.
Vacancy means rentals, small
like a pinto, smooth
ceramic down to the base
that's tasteless, odorless,
and formless as a baby born
in its nakedness, last days
apocalypse, never been a
materialist, can't stand it,
soul stranded, clinging
to nothing—see, empty handed.

August 29, 2015

Hear Ye, Hear Ye

When tired of standing
 take a seat and when tired
  of laying stand on your feet,
   but when tired of breathing comes
    no relief.
No surrender,
 because in the game
  of life there's no losers
   or winners, a situation
    viewed critical outcome pivotal,
but livable and when
 taken to serious causes
  delirious feelings of mixed
   conviction and the only relief
    comes from total submission.

November 11, 2015

Determination

All I need is one shot
the size of a dot, a small
crack or tear in the seam
and watch me turn a
nightmare into a sweet dream
'cause all I need is just
a little not a lot for I
can take a story and turn
it into a movie plot a
bestselling book all the
way to the top, just a
speck to be correct, from
a science project to a
billion-dollar object,
there's no stopping it
up and down like
hydraulics, my determination
is flawless.

February 7, 2016

My Finale

            It's been well spoken
even better said,
            ink depleted and
seldomly repeated,
            a configuration of sentences
turned into phrases
            called paragraphs,
a book filled with pages,
            literature at its best,
but when compress calls for less,
            a scholastic archive of
opinions generated on paper
            from antonyms to
synonyms from a mind that's willing
            them, a trinity,
but to me it's just plain old poetry.

            July 23, 2015

Smoke

The smell is so evident
that you would say it must be
weed, but it's the words I wrote
that burn like leaves,
giving off clouds of white smoke
that I inhale as I read, causing
me to choke, I can't breathe
as the page sets ablaze, but too
high to be afraid, because it's
the powers within me that crumble
the mystery of life like
ashes at my feet, blessing
my soul to the harmony
of its destiny,
where ignorance is easy to
swallow makes it hard for
enlightenment to follow as drops
trickle off my lips
like saliva, but
I don't bother to wipe my mouth,
because the truth is worth
talking about.

September 16, 2016

We Don't Exist

You think that's love you feel, food you're eating or air you're breathing, think again because we don't exist. Blinded by ignorance and seeking spiritual deliverance, but who are we kidding. We stumbled into the land of the forbidden, where a lie is like a snake and fools get bitten, we don't exist and if you think so show me where it's written, I insist, but you won't find it, because we don't exist.

January 26, 2016

The Poetic Master

When my eyes close
my world becomes two-fold,
a platform for my dissertation
of words in a world where speech
is not the form of communication,
where I comprise and utilize
words into sentences, the nemesis
of making you feel this takes
a realist not a gimmick,
but a true artist who writes
from the heart of his soul
and takes delight in the essence
of God that grows like a single
rose in the garden of my mind
surrounded by weeds on a vine
that want it to die, but
it survives by the weapons of
the divine, the pen and the paper
develop skills that appear
unbelievably real and becomes
intoxicated by the fumes
of his blood that spills upon
the pages of what he feels.
The last of the last
born under the seventh seal
and the right hand of God that
wrote the book of the dead
with a monsoon of thoughts
raining down on his head,
he offers his words to the
world as sweet raisin bread.

April 2, 2016

Stagnation

No motion not even
 a notion, not logical
  to speak nor impossible
   to be when all life cease
    to exist not dead, but
     frozen in God's consciousness.
    A frame that hangs on
   the wall in the hall of
  eternity, a collection
 of memories over centuries
and millenniums to infinity.

February 3, 2016

The In Between

It's that tiny gap of nothingness
 that happens so quick, very
  few will ever notice it,
complete emptiness and absolute
 stillness, where only the soul is
  the witness.
That split second of silence, peace
 and tranquility that lies between
  every action and thought of
   humanity.
It is said to be the place where our
 true self hides its face behind
  the clouds of the mind,
but if you seek, sunshine is what
 you shall find.

August 25, 2016

A Passing Thought

Just a while
 before they fade,
  Just a glimpse
   then it's gone away,
    Never here to stay
     back and forth
      like waves across the
       bay. Thoughts
        that's what they are
         that comes and goes,
          some dense and others
           shallow as they hang
            in the gallows
             waiting for the end
              just to fade away once
               again.

February 13, 2016

A Year

A
year is
twelve months with
twelve names, twelve astrological
signs means twelve symbols that form
a chain, a 360-degree
cycle, fifty-two
weeks, seven days all
in a line equals three-hundred-
and-sixty-five with the four seasons
in mind just before
it rewinds, except
when it takes a
leap every
three,
plus one day, four years
then it's complete
and
what a year it will
be!

April 2, 2016

Outside The Box

So dramatic
like politics and aristocratics,
airport delays and bad
habits, the whole
universe is yours so reach
out and grab it, touch the sky
and feel the fabric.
A new day begins with
sunbeams as the birds sings
God the King, so merciful
and mighty with only a thought
in the instance of a passing
breath, the in between
not behind the scene,
because there's nothing else.

February 6, 2016

Kundalini

She is the beauty of the night,
the secret love of my life,
oh, why do you hide from my
sight for you are the passion
that burns in my desire to
spiritually rise higher.
Few have laid eyes upon
her elegance, the queen
of inner dominance with a heart
full of love in great abundance.
She comes and goes as she pleases
with every breath that flows
through my mouth and out of
my nose as she graces my soul
with her presence and when
we embrace it's heaven,
stimulating the seven points of
my chi, causing my body to
shake and shiver from her
energy, while leaving me
dreamy eyed, but not
surprised.

March 30, 2016

So Tired

So tired
 of waking up in the
   middle of the night with
     bloody knuckles from a dream fight,
So tired
 that I no longer have
   the strength to pray,
So tired
 I can't even ask God
   to take the pain away,
So tired
 I can't even cry
   just want to close my
     eyes and hope to die,
So tired
 that I just want to rest
   in peace, but the question
     on whether I gave my best
       just keeps on tormenting me.

February 6, 2016

The Simple Life

I
have hopes and dreams,
but
the reality is I settle for the
lesser things. You know,
food, clothing, and shelter
and whatever else
I may need, the basic necessities
nothing out of greed,
because I fell in love
with the simple life,
only a slice not the whole
pie, just enough to
get me by.

August 25, 2016

Anything

As we go about our day
anything can come our way,
from this to that
all in a blink of an eye,
somebody will be born and
somebody will die, but
who's to say which way life
will sway, the ifs,
ands, and maybes are all
possibilities of maladies,
here today, gone tomorrow,
smiles of joy or tears of sorrow,
the pain of expectation
has no gain, for
anything never stays the same
and everything is
guaranteed to change,
as to what that might be
is between you and
destiny.

August 25, 2016

Change

Yes, I'm an addict
addicted to bad habits.
Alcohol and drugs I got to
have it.
Yeah, I know
it's a temporary fix,
but it takes me away from
the bullshit that's why I'm
always looking for the next
hit.
I know I need a change,
bit it's hard to explain,
so much rage and pain that
I just want to get away, no
blaming just changing along
the way.

February 24, 2016

Anonymous

My identity is
anonymous, I have
no name, but I'm not
ashamed for all that
remains are the artifacts of
whips and chains, haunted by
the foul odor of decaying flesh and
blood stains, ominous for centuries
that's the misery of my ancestry.
slavery crossed out of history
shows no sympathy and
anonymous as it might be,
I'm the mini "G" in
God's legacy, so if
you know God then
my identity is
no mystery,
but to the
ignorant
I remain
anonymously.

February 21, 2016

Blissness

Don't be alarmed
when you hear this,
I'm in the state
of blissness,
mental happiness
and
physical fitness
surrounded
by the aura of God,
where the soul
is the witness.

March 5, 2016

Been Around the World

From the Great Lakes
of the United States,
I swam to the ports
of Singapore to the clay
huts of Ecuador
then across the Red Sea to
the meridian just to see the
blue waters of the Caribbean,
barefooted I traveled the
hot sands of Niger to Zaire, no
passport to enter Malawi sent
back to Zimbabwe, had to work
my mojo in the Congo just to
get to Fiji before I was deported
to Chile fell in love with Bolivia,
but I got a wife named Syria,
neighbors in Liberia next door
to Algeria to the white sands
of Pakistan then rode the camel
like a mad man to Afghanistan
just to meet the native people
called Africans in a ceremony of the
Sudanese chewing the cocoa leaves,
hypnotized by the high,
what a ride back to the
stateside.

February 15, 2016

Suicidal Tendencies

I was mentally distraught,
but you heard me not.
I told you my name,
but you forgot.
I called you many times,
but you paid me no mind.
I was drowning in sorrow,
but you threw me no life line.
So out of despair,
I cried hoping you would care,
but I finally realized
that no one was there
and I did what I thought
I would never dare.
So, I'm no longer the object
of neglect, but rather
the subject
of regret.

September 13, 2016

Can We Come Together

Can we come together
and forget about all that
we know, I just want
to hold you so I can
feel the essence of
life flow.
Can we come together
for the better and not for
the worse, putting down
the weapons of jealousy,
greed, and envy that makes
our souls victims of misery
and spreads like a disease
not only in us, but throughout
the world communities.
Can we come together,
because I know you feel
the same deep down inside,
but you feel ashamed so
you rather lie than
to even try.
Can we come together
and share our tears
that reflects our pain
and suffering in this world,
that makes life not
worth living, but our
love for each other
is worth giving.
Can we come together
as civilized human
beings without all

*the disparities in
color and just love
one another.*

December 6, 2007

Breath After Breath

Life starts
 with a breath
  and continue breath
   after breath until death,
    where nothing is taken
     and all is left.

September 30, 2016

The Seed Trilogy

One day
I was walking home
 and found a seed, so I
  planted it in the backyard
   out of curiosity. Months later
it grew into a garden,
 so I gave the food to those
  who were starving and they
   fed their children until they were
    grown, then sent them out, but not
alone with a pocket full of
 seeds to be sown. They
  planted them here, there,
   and everywhere. Now,
millions of years old
 those same seeds feed
  the entire globe.

August 26, 2016

A Dangerous Mind

Backstage is taking the back seat in your
reality, seeing what you see in duality.
A spectator in the arena of your thoughts,
trying not to get lost in the drama of
your mind. Where your heart is
filled with black clouds of hate,
that's why it's always night and
never day. When it rains, it
floods your brain with all
sorts of crazy things. The
aggression, depression and
low self-esteem make you
hurt others or yourself
by any means, but in
no way a part of my
reality, because I'm
behind the scene.

September 16, 2016

Queen Bee

They call her
 queen bee because
  she leads the colony,
   born under royalty to
    a force of an army that's
     totally dedicated to protecting
      her every interest, where making
       honey is the business and the
        exit is the same as the entrance,
       attack the hive and you will see
      their loyalty to survive or
     die, this is the side of
    nature we don't normally
   see, where there's no
  discrimination,
 just equality.

September 13, 2016

The
T
H
E
O
R
E
M

is the serum
that will set you free,
for fools let their ignorance
guide them mentally.
Where only the truth
can bring you back to reality,
for death awaits in
the valley.
Fear not and Forget not
the verse of the bread
and wine.
Open your mind
to the words of the
divine, sweeter than
pure honey or grapes
on a vine.

February 11, 2017

I Don't Want

I don't want,
 the flies associated
   with the bullshit in trying
     to give explanations to cover
       up your fabrications.
I don't want,
 the fame or fortune
   nor the spoils of war from
     the rich or any of the materialistic
       things called lavish that cause's people
         to act like savage's
I don't want
 the blood stains
   from dead remains
     or feeling ashamed,
       because I was the blame.
I don't want,
 the woe's of the status quo
   in being a family man with
     kid's or an endless amount
       of so called friends.
I don't want
 the attachments to
   illusions that cause's so
     much confusion or the stigma
       of living life right or wrong
         in being over zealous or head strong.
I don't want,
 any kind of association
   by any mean's, just complete
     isolation so I can breathe.

May 4, 2015

Never Been In Love

I never had the chance to prove that I
can be true or the opportunity to hold
a woman's hand and say I do. Those
emotions never came into play, but
that's not to say it won't happen
someday. For now I can only imagine,
some say being in love is wonderful
and mystical as magic, but
others say it can be a story
ending tragic. Where broken
hearts come and go in the
traffic of life's flow.

February 13, 2017

The Human Odyssey

A testament of one's
journey, a story
with no allegory, the uncut
symmetry of a flawless
legacy, described
in a pedigree of abstract
realities, the sediments of
thought based upon the
rudiments of life, where
we only live as is and
never twice, the human
colony of biology, yes!
The odyssey is what we be,
a trinity of life, death,
and God's infinite
energy.

March 11, 2016

I Cry

I cry,
because I did not
understand what it was to
be a man. I abandoned my life like
a sinking ship and watched my emotions drown in it.

I cry,
because I did not fight
physically and refused to swim
mentally. Therefore, I died
spiritually.

I cry,
because I should no longer
exist, hollow as a cocoon after
the butterfly has left it.

I cry,
because I have been living the
life of a fool in not realizing that
I was still very much alive and if
that wasn't true then explain these
tears falling from my eyes, that's why

I cry.

February 28, 2017

Anticipation

Damn!
It's killing me,
but I love it like a novelty,
like an author's delight –
trilogy, all this anxiety got
me on the edge of my seat
feeling jittery, waiting
and watching anxiously, while
thinking consciously about
the other possibility,
for expectation is like a
wishing well, but who will
kiss and tell, some will
succeed and some will fail,
what then when reality
settles in will you break or bend,
twist or turn, just another
hard lesson learned, that happens
over and over again, a
fifty/fifty blend
with a different type
of end.

March 4, 2016

Devil

Since the beginning
of time you have concocted
an evil image in the people's
mind. All the calamities and
miseries of humanity you have placed
upon this shrine. You gave it a name
and for everything bad it took the blame.
Yet, it's your evil desires and deeds
that cause each other hearts to
bleed. Where covering up your
devilish intentions is why
this myth of a devil was
ever invented.

February 28, 2017

Self-Inflicted

I feel possessed by a python
never been famous, icon.
My addiction is self-infliction.
Mental state controlled by drugs of
prescription, evidence of self-
mutilation certified mental
patient. Suicide I tried, but I
never died, yes, I'm insane and
hurting myself is the aim.
Excuses fall like the rain,
justification, no one to blame.
Too much pressure causes
radical measures. The
harder I pull, the less I
gain, the weight of life
is an ounce to a grain.
My self-esteem is through
the floor, agonizing
pain to the core with
no will to live anymore,
but I forgot to mention
that my words are full
of contradiction!

July 7, 2015

Technical Difficulties

*Sorry,
but life is full of
technicalities,
laws, rules, policies
shortcomings and fallacies.
Attacking
our mental state
with assaults and
batteries, causing
unconscious casualties.
Tragedy after Tragedy,
misery on top of misery,
this is the totality
of the rivalry
between insanity
and sanity. Where
The gravity of the
human reality is nothing
more than vanity.*

March 9, 2017

Kiss the Sky

Clear blue skies
cause me to squint
my eyes to block out
the sunlight,
just to open them to
the night, brisk, cool
and crisp, looking up and
blowing the moon a kiss,
a slight tease of
a breeze shakes the leaves
on the trees, jealousy, do I
sense a star's insecurity.
That's why I kiss the
sky, emotional vibes make
the clouds cry to hear the
echoes of my hellos
just before I say goodbye, this
is why I kiss the sky!

March 8, 2016

Life

The meaning of life has many different
definitions, most of which is based on
one's living.
So, is life just the mere fact that you're
breathing or is it about achieving.
Your existence as well as mine mean
little in the minds of others and
what about love, it's constantly being
swept underneath the rug.
Many claim life to be so precious, but
they live so reckless.
Where is the value of life placed and why?
Do some base it on the color of your face.
Why? Is money, power and respect so
important to us and tell me who can you
share it with if there's no one to trust.
For some religion is a way out of the
world and into the truth, but without
dedication that becomes quite hard too.
So, you seriously need to ask yourself what
is life? And what it means to you, because
I am not judging or suggesting what you
should or should not do, I am only letting
you know what you reap is
what you sow.

Words of Wisdom

Stand in boldness
 like a blade of grass,
  then take solace in the warmth
   of the morning sun's grasp.
Be not ignorant to the
 knowledge of self,
  those who are fear death.
Inhale the universe's breath
 then exhale the reminisce
  of self.
Be as the wise
 and keep your eyes on
  the prize, for God is the
   best kept secret not yet
    realized.
Be humble in your
 religious beliefs and
  stumble not into grief
   for the fruits of pride
    brings no relief.
Show me imperfection and
 I will show you a fool
  who can't be resurrected.
Temptation weakens
 the soul and
  for the price of an ounce
   of gold many are sold.
To love nothing
 is impossible, but
  to love everything
   is your destiny of
    an obstacle.

March 16, 2015

Some Time This, Some Time That

Sometime I feel glad and sometime I feel sad, sometime I'm full of gratitude and sometime I'm just rude, sometime I'm wrong and sometime I'm right, sometime I feel like giving up and sometime I feel lifted up, sometime I feel at peace and sometime I feel guilty, sometime I feel pleasure and sometime I feel pain, sometime I wish it would snow and sometime it just rain, sometime I'm smart and sometime I play the fool, sometime I appreciate and sometime I hate, sometime I say "yes" and sometime I say "no", sometime I say maybe and sometime I say are you crazy, sometime whether we like it or not things just get tied up in a knot. Yet, nothing remains the same and everything changes with time. For each day of our lives, we travel a new path based on our spiritual need, it may be gaining knowledge or helping others in need, nothing is never for nothing it always lead to something.

When My Eyes Close

When my eyes close,
 the light goes pitch black
as the subconscious backtracks,
 the mind switches back and
thoughts become a racetrack
 that attacks like vandals, close
doors without handles, brain
 cells scramble to form mental
    pictures in sporadic flashes, but
too dramatic in fashion, so vivid,
 so real you can feel the clashing
    of light become colorful scenes
of dreams or nightmares filled
 with screams, then suddenly
everything's serene, no more dreams,
only beams of the spiritual
 me is left, one breath away
from death as the smell of
 rose petals arouse the nose,
but only when my eyes are closed.

July 31, 2015

Love Is Pt. 2

Love is God, love is life, love is you, love is me, love is the entire universe collectively, love is understanding, love is true, love is light, but so is night, love is peace, love is tranquility, love is forgiving, love is harmony, love is infinity, love is unmistakable, love is uncontainable, love is spirituality, love is vitality, love is divine, love is faith, love is the opposite of hate, love is emotional, love is all creation in its highest state, love is so great, love is beautiful, love is patience, love is revelation, love is the core of energy forever more and the key to heaven's door.

Change Pt. 2

If you want change
then make it, bad habits
break it, but don't
mistake it as easy, believe
me many have tried
and many have died
in the process, some
by suicide from all the
stress, others got
arrested, we can bear
witness to this, but starting
now failure is not an
option, it's your willingness
and your need to succeed
that will set you free, taking
command is making a stand,
because change is nothing if
you do nothing, so the plan is to
do something and that
something is being methodical
in putting down the drugs
and the alcohol bottle.

February 25, 2016

"The City of the Dead"

   As the snow begins to rise in the morning skies,
a breeze from across the sea stirs up dust
forming debris on the earth's crust.
   On the wings of wind gray clouds roll in, and
a drizzle there a drizzle everywhere then
suddenly heavy rain against the window
pane.
   That sound made me reminisce about my
loved ones that I so dearly miss and the
times we spent together on days like this.
   I became saddened from those once lost thoughts
as they ran through my head and decided to
pay my respects to them in a place called
"the city of the dead."
   I grabbed my raincoat and umbrella that
lay resting on the rack near the door, took two
flowers from the garden then ran back to get
more.
   No car, because it wasn't that far. I preferred
to walk and talk with my own thoughts of past
memories from long ago.
   As I reached this place of rest the tall brick
walls caught my interest with its steel
black gates that lay opened at the
entrance.
   Overhead, you could see the trees
hanging like human limbs blowing in
the wind as the rain made a tapping
sound as it fell down upon the leaves
creating small streams on the ground that
made not a sound as the water flowed
down.

When I passed the entranceway the stillness took my breath away, for I knew this very day that I finally had the chance to say what I always wanted to say.

Where time and space mattered no more, I stood between two worlds, the living and the dead, to break bread with both as I could feel a heavenly host standing close guiding me by the hand through this strange land.

There were many rows of headstones where souls once danced the dance of life and roamed the night, but that was now gone and only bones remained with dates and names engraved.

Suddenly, I stopped and my hands dropped as I noticed the family plot and even through the rain I could see the name.

I fell to my knees and placed the flowers upon their chest where they rest and said, "Oh, Lord please let my prayers be heard if not my last word."

When I opened my eyes, day had turned into night and all that I could see was a blinding light, and out of the light came a hand that gently pulled me within.

Inside this light was a sense of total peace as serenity engulfed me from my head down to my feet, while being surrounded by bodies with faces that I recognized of past relatives who died.

And a voice said, "You have done what many would like in a place where the living and the dead unite. So, say your peace and let the dead be for in time you will be with us for eternity.

For death is not the end, but a new time that begins. Where there's no fleshly skin, only the light that shines within."

With those words I spoke my peace and then suddenly fell into a deep sleep to be awoken in my bed shaking my head.

As I gathered my thoughts I said to myself, am I alive or dead, but believing that I was just dreaming as I heard the door bell ringing.

Jumping up from the bed, I strolled to the door almost slipping on water that laid at the door, do I need to say anymore!

August 24, 2007

A Ghost of a Man

I'm empty as a shell,
dust in the hand, so don't
inhale or you will breathe
me in.
Hollow like a fossil of a
human being as I gaze at
my own reflection, I can't
believe what I'm seeing.
A dead man walking,
soulless that means lifeless
like a zombie, no heart
beat.
But I wasn't always like
this, I got served up a
bad dish called malice
and prejudice.
Now I am just as useless
as an old coat in need
of a host, a ghost of a man
exiled to a foreign land
to die on my own all
alone.

April 14, 2015

Memories

Like ripples in the sea
each one holds a story called
a memory, still pictures like
moving figures that dance around
in the mind constantly reminding
us of past times. Some heavy or dense
others light or shallow like a morning
mist passing in the wind as it blows
with no end and like everything in life
it passes with time, but memories are
passed times recorded in the mind from
birth to death and beyond the grave these
memories will forever be engraved to
see; but not to be for it's all history
and to turn is to learn from a back
view for whatever happens here and now
lies on you, and like footprints in the sand
so is memories when held in the hand only for
a moment do we actually own it, before tossing
it back into the sea of memories where its
purpose can't be explained; but like pictures in
a frame you can see everything, your every experience
written in your mind, an autobiography of past times.

The Grit and the Grind

The grit is the rough and rugged
from the walk of time
breeded in pride with
only the will to survive
that is the force of the spirit
that lies behind the mind
and
the grind is the particles of life
redefined, broken down to
its last compound, reformed
and reshaped, so make no
mistake the grit and
the grind was meant
to make us all
great.

May 10, 2015

Give Me The Strength

When your feet stumble and your hands
shake to the point where you're about
to break wait!, listen and
look. For motivation is lurking somewhere
around for that call of a sound when
someone's down.
It appears in an instance with sheer
determination and constant persistence
giving you 100% of pure adrenaline. Not
just a mental conception, but a physical
acceptance to a source of energy that is the
remedy to any obstacle that lie in your
path. Pure power that you're able to grasp and
harness for your own use anything
less is no excuse.
For God has provided us with the tools
to overcome, spiritual resilience from his
kingdom. Therefore, keep your head up
and fight with all your might. For to fail
is not to try and in a state of depression
is where you will die.

A Second Class Citizen

God divided the Red Sea,
  but who or what divides humanity.
    A second class citizen, what a
      misery of a reality that I thought
        was history, but obviously
          I was blind-sided by my own mind,
            where no love of any kind will
              I ever find, I'm no animal
                just an ordinary individual, see
              touch me I'm physical.

August 1, 2015

The Most Beauteous Thing

It's a blessing to even be able to conceive
the thought of having a baby and to take
it likely would be crazy.
Something so small, tender and of pure
innocence and to be a witness to this
gift is magnificent.
Spiritual perfection at its best.
Another soul about to embark upon
a quest.
A single glance of those big stunning
eyes will make you cry with joy as
you see yourself in this baby girl or
boy.
You will hold your baby up towards
the sky with tears in your eyes giving
thanks to God with a voice that roars
like thunder in great wonder for this
small bundle.
Saying, what can be greater than life
as your words echo through the night
a sign of grace in every way, a
miracle here to stay.
With a smile that is so precious
and undefiled and with eyes that
are full of love and gratitude that
sparkle with great charity to no
disparity.
The flesh of your flesh with heaven's
breath brought forth by pregnancy
is another legacy on the throne of
humanity.

The Supreme

I'm just a silhouette
In God's dance – a
pirouette, a gleam in His
sunbeam, the little me within
the big "G", but without the
rhapsody in living religiously,
but I practice the truth
rigorously and whole heartedly,
with integrity and honesty,
that's the best part of me
and together we are God's
recipe, the ingredients
of his existence, every breath
is the evidence, nothing is
irrelevant, so hail to the King,
the always and forever,
The Supreme.

March 2, 2016

No Discipline

Why? can't I take heed to good information
 instead of causing complications that results
  in altercations.
Why? can't I learn from my mistakes to
 better myself instead of hurting myself.
Why? do I continue to bash my head against
 the brick wall and watch myself fall time
  and time again.
Maybe I do what I do because I choose to.
 I never was humble I guess that's why I'm
  quick to stumble.
I love to fight whether wrong or right
 I don't care about curfews I stay out
  all night.
Rules and laws are for fools, they make
 them and I break them every chance I get
  because I'm not afraid to bite the bullet.
I don't care about felony cases; I been to
 prison twice and they already know me on
  first name basis.
Some say that I am a fool and others
 say that I am crazy yet it doesn't phase
  me in fact it amazes me how I stay in
the center of their lives, just
 because I'm not living right.
The difference is they do theirs in
 the dark and I do mine's in the
  light;
I don't care about right or wrong
 because I'm headstrong even though
  deep down inside I know I'm dead
   wrong.

Just Anybody

Everybody is somebody
    somewhere
even if you know nobody
    'cause
everybody is everybody
    so
anybody can be someone,
    but
no one can be everyone,
    because
the somewhat is the only one,
    so
who's who if you ain't you
    and
I'm not me, so how do I
    define
myself, that's easy, call me
    Just Anybody.

March 12, 2016

Retrospect

How many graves have been dug to bury
the dead too many to count off the top
of your head, what about the lives that
have been shattered to pieces leaving
behind a foul odor of feces, why can't
we just live and forget past events
then hanging onto it like a national
monument, when we kill like animals
out of instincts never taking the time
to think spilling precious blood like
water down a sink, but crime and violence
amuses many; but when speaking the
truth you can't find any, yet you celebrate
the dead with days on a calendar and
burning candles, but destroy life like a
vandal as you scrutinize with an evil
eye those just trying to survive just because
you have everything money can buy as you
claim to be a good person, but that's hard
to believe when you're sitting back thinking
of ways to deceive a situation so sad in
a world that's gone mad, but I guess some things
in life can't be or won't be resolved as it
continues to evolve and maybe
that's the way it's supposed to be. A
cold-hearted reality.

The Journey Within

Two million miles
to Graceland
surrounded by mental wastelands,
a reality
we must all face then
as I descend
again to hell again, I failed
again, so I must die again
just to rise again to
find the inner path
again, so let the
journey begin again from where
I last ended then, not to
sin again, damn,
I did it again!

September 22, 2016

I Know Your Struggle

See, I went through the same thing
and played the same game.
Chasing materialistic things like
money and fame, but in the end what
do we really gain, absolutely nothing.

Trying to satisfy your every need
always turn to greed while envy and
jealousy will have you chasing dreams,
losing touch with reality as you end up
like a soldier on the front line in the
middle of war time.

So, I know your struggle it costed me
a great deal of trouble, for which I'm
still paying the cost, but I'm no
longer lost.

I wasted too many years and tears
worrying about how others saw me, which
caused me to become someone else instead
of being myself.

I let the world shape and mold
my mind with ignorance taking my
     innocence and replacing
it with stupidity making me guilty.

Crime became my best friend and
it was a do or die situation to the
end and even though it's been years
ago it still seems like yesterday

because it still shows upon my
resumé.

So, I am not looking for your sympathy,
but know it's no longer in me to
hurt other people and unlike a movie
there won't be a sequel.

For with each passing day, I'm finding
new ways to better myself.

I'm no longer looking up, but looking down
keeping my feet on the ground, this way, I
will never forget where I been or where I want
to be which helps me see clearly by keeping the
truth near me.

Soul Anthem

(1) The mind is like a glutton,
a shirt without a button.
   Open for human consumption that
      leads to mental corruption causing
         chaotic solutions.
            (2) Answers become polluted and twisted,
damn you blank, sorry you
   missed it.

            (3) From deviant behavior
to criminal activity,
   for a second of heaven to a lifetime
      of misery.
            (4) What is sanity?
When you speak of such vanity,
   humanity is like a canopy.
      covering you with lies,
         these are the horror stories
            that change lives.
            (5) I don't mean to depress you,
but the truth is like tissue,
   wiping up every false issue.
            (6) Sensitivity does nothing for the soul,
there's nothing worse than watching
   a fool grow old.
            (7) How many victims has misconception
created?
   Only the mentally strong shall be
      vindicated.
            (8) This battle is of spiritual principalities
you can't see,
   no one is the enemy,

   your fight is with yourself
    mentally.
       (9) The world can be like a jungle
sometimes,
 so rumble, rumble,
  young lion!

November 11, 2014

Remember The Times

We were two of a kind
like grapes on a vine
and wherever you went, I followed close behind.

We were so young and I
can't believe all the crazy things we done.

There was much laughter, fun
and joy, especially unwrapping
those new Christmas toys.

Whether right or wrong,
I always tagged along.

You would lie for me
and I would lie for you,
there was no limit to the things we would do.

Remember, how mom would make
us go out and find switches to
beat our behinds, we brought back the
smallest we could find. I was glad for the
belt, because those switches left welts.

You used to run like your butt
was on fire, and after chasing
you she was always tired.
That's why, I let you go first,
because that was the worst.

Then Mom would say,
I still love my babies

for that vanilla ice cream
and blueberry pie quickly
dried the eyes.

And even though it was con,
it always worked like a charm.

Then, we would joke ourselves
to sleep, just to wake up to another
day causing Mom more agony.

You got your bike before mine,
so I had to ride the handle bars
and remember the bike stunts,
I still got the scars.

And what about those old karate
flicks and how we used to go outside
and try to do it.
You were Bruce Lee and I was Bruce Li,
Saturday Night Live and my favorite
dance the electric slide.

The backyard brawls. I was
Junk Yard Dog and you were
Jimmy "Superfly" Snucka.
WWF's finest every Saturday
morning around nineous.

And what about Halloween
and how we would chase the girls
and make them scream.

Remember, the game hide and seek,
catch a girl before she reach the tree,

it was K-I-S-S-I-N-G.

Those were the good old days and
remember the clothes there was
no suede.
Flannel shirts, bell bottoms,
Converse and apple jack hats
with the feather pin
clips hanging off the back.

Skates with metal wheels
or the football helmets with
the two bar grills.

Families were tight back then,
but look at us now we're not
even close as friends.

But, you're still my brother and
you will always be, and even
though we're grown and you have
a family of your own. Never forget
how we used to be, because all we
have is those memories.

MICHAEL WAYNE BRYANT

The Humanimal Kingdom

Demonic possession without redemption, go
Animalistic for instance, a fight of animals
on animals is consistent in relation to
Human existence. Where gorilla's against
monkey's is forbidden, lion's move swiftly
Hunted by the grizzly ends bloody.
Making the ground muddy, because
There's nothing cuddly about the
King cobra when it stands erect
As the black widow spun her net.
The tiger prey on its next subject,
that elephants never forget
causing stampede's of buffalo's
running though the gallows.
Gators lie in the shallows, black
Mamba, in the teeth of a
Piranha, hush, wolves hide
In the under-brush. No victim
is a plus, but it still happens
soon enough, because in
the drama of the Jungle of
life. Humans fight just to
survive another night, only
to die in the end less
and win less fight.

August 3, 2015

Our Father

Our Father, hallowed be your name,
I come to you in despair and shame
Oh, what wretchedness I have
brought upon myself. Now, I have
nothing left, but bitterness and
pain with no one to blame.

I bow down before you and your
kingdom of grace and confess that
my life is a waste. I have no right
to ask of your forgiveness, because
you have always been there it was me
who didn't care.

Now, I swear upon my own soul
that I have traveled the wrong road,
leading me to a dead end and wishing
that I could start my life over again.

So much sin, it's coming out of my skin
and now it's destroying me from within,
like a parasite. I no longer have the strength
or will to fight.

I have reached the point of no
return and I must receive what I
deserve for denying and forsaking you
this is what I must go through. If I
had seeked the kingdom of heaven, I
would not have lived the life of a felon.

Now, I have nailed myself to the cross,

whereas Jesus had already paid the cost.
My blood washes away no sins it only
falls to the ground, dries up and blows
away in the wind.

The world have no sympathy for my
suffering, I can only see them smile as
the fowl's approach upon me. Not as my
friends, but as my enemies to harm me.

So, now I stand before those people and
material things that I put before you as
death approaches like a tsunami. Hence,
I mourn in my own misery, because I know
horrible things will come near me.

Surely, if there is a hell I am
headed there with the clashing of
my teeth along with my flesh burning
and falling off of me, as brimstone
bursts out of my chest and in the
valley of death is where I will rest.

I have not much time left, for I am
almost at my last breath. The fowls
have plucked out my eyes and without
tears I can not cry as death awaits
for me to die.

Therefore, I cry out to you "our father",
with much regret for my payment of
death is sorrowfully accepted. For
I blinded myself in the ways of the
world and refused to follow your word.

I choose the darkness instead of the light
and my soul is the sacrifice. So, from the bottom
of my heart I can now truly say that you are
what you say you are the alpha and the omega,
the beginning and the end.

Only, if I had the time
I would say I'm sorry,
I'm sorry, I'm sorry
for my sins, time and time
again.

Listen Up

Take heed and
listen to your parents
and the elderly,
because experience pays the salary
and nothing is gained without a mutual
exchange that's the reality in
receiving advice that might
save your life, so save
yourself some trials and
tribulations and in time you will
learn to have patience, so
listen up instead of complaining,
because common sense is
lacking while ignorance
is gaining.

September 13, 2016

The Visionary

Contrary to popular beliefs and myths,
I bring you the story of a visionist.

Once, there lived a man with the power of
vision, not considered talented or gifted
as he possessed the power to predict the
next hour.

He practiced it to a craft then mastered
it down to a single element as he used
it to help others made him benevolent.

His body would shake and shiver when a
vision was being delivered. Then his pupils
would dilate in such a way that no light
could escape causing his retina to magnify
his eyes like laser beams scanning the scene
between time and space until it stood still
in one place.

Then his mind would formulate pictures from
the particles of fate gathered by the fabric
of time multiplied seven times. To come face
to face with destiny.

Motion exploded without a sound
while holding its position to avoid
a collision with his mental thoughts
that traveled like meteorites into
the night at a speed faster than
light.

And like film on a reel your future
was revealed like a prophecy unsealed,
giving him the power to see how your
next hour of life would be lived.

With such a gift most would have taken
advantage of it yet he took no pleasure
in it. He said, whatever happens is the
result of his own choices. Therefore,
whether he knew or not it could only be
delayed not stopped.

And even though this poem is fictional, what
if you did possess the power to make your
future predictable? Would you change
the hands of time, just a question
in the back of my mind on whether
or not you would cross that line.

Desperado

You're hard pressed for the material things
so your gain comes by any means,
you fight for crumbs like city park
bums, lurking like rats in the dark
for the bare minimum makes you
a criminal, because feverish
minds take whatever they
can find, a pitch black
state of mind, read the
sign, but there it goes
again, that feeling
from within leading you to
another <u>dead end</u>.

September 13, 2016

When Sunshine Turns To Rain

They say out of the darkness came the light,
   for when the sun rises it's a sweet delight.
   Over the horizon it be peeping slowly,
   creeping higher and higher
   until it reach its empire.
The rays it generate illuminate the skies
   making everything visible to the eye.
   Its strength is unmeasurable
   and the sight of its presence is
   unforgettable.
You have no choice but to recognize its power
   for twelve or more hours;
   while it showers one side of the earth
   as the other side awaits its birth
   allowing every living organism to do its work.
The heat massages your muscles and joints
   with warmth,
   causing your skin to perspire giving you
   the motivation to carry out your desires.
It embellishes your flesh with vitamin D
   changing your whole chemistry
   and even though too much can drain
   you physically, without it where
   would humanity be.
So, dare not complain, but enjoy it all
   the same. For as the day comes
   to a close, the sun makes one last
   impression before it goes, like when
   a miner strikes gold the clouds unload
   with rain cooling off the earth
   after a long day.
Out of the clouds comes drops after drops,

so many it seems as though it
   will never stop.
Sometimes it brings high winds, thunder
   and lightning. Sending vibrations
   through the ground with a sound
   that causes the hairs on your neck
   to stand up erect and from an old
   cliché some will say, "God is hard
   at it."
Yet, this is not always the case and sometimes
   rain comes in a whole different way.
   It may last for hours or even days
   leaving the earth covered in a haze,
   causing condensation due to the
   saturation of rain and finally
   evaporation that is a process
   linked together like a chain.
As I sometime find myself in its mist
   with drops falling upon my lips,
   which is like a sweet kiss from nature,
   but is tantalizing, because it
   disappears like vapors.
For each droplet finds its place and in a
   short time it covers my entire face,
   as if to say you are now cleansed
   from your sins within.
Then, I close my eyes and when I open
   them nothing seems to be the same.
   Some say it's all in my mind
   and others say I'm going insane,
but I tell you there is something special
about sunshine and rain.

Sensory

The sight in my eyes
  keeps the fire of desire
    burning within my heart
  and
the touch of my hands
  against the surface guides
   me through the dark,
     as
my ears let me hear the
  slightest of sounds, alerting
   me to any danger lurking
    around,
     for
my sense of smell gives me
directions, improvise and
  make corrections when
     necessary,
just so my tongue can savor
  the taste of the fruits
   of my labor.

March 12, 2016

Greatness

Greatness can't be
 weighed in pounds
  or ounces
   Like gold
    or measured by material wealth
     to have and to hold.
      Nor by accomplishments of any kind.
       A false perception of the mind,
        believed to be in all that
         we achieve.
          Greatness is the seed
           of humanity in all degrees
            of creation.
             For it is always in the
              making,
               manifestation after
                manifestation, so
                 welcome to
                  Greatness.

October 22, 2017

You Are

You are the opposite of me
pure beauty in its highest degree.
A candle-lit dinner by the sea,
a memory that will last for eternity.
The birds sing in your presence
as the clouds cover your head like
an umbrella.
Your hair sways back and forth
like waves in the ocean
from the slightest breeze that
keeps it all in motion.
Fragrant aromas flow from your
skin
like a thousand kits blowing in
the wind, dancing the dance of
romance as we walk hand in hand.
For you are my woman
and I'm your man.
You are my everything and
much more,
someone I love and adore
for evermore.
You are, you are, my shining star.

May 17, 2010

A Matter Of Opinion

Beauty don't
exist, it's
a myth a matter
of opinion.
Just words rolling
off of the lips
or perception
on top of perception
with no ending
only questions with
no beginning.
True beauty comes
from within and within
is where it remains,
because it can't be
recognized or described
much less explained.

October 23, 2017

Autumn Breeze

Watch the wind blow
  as the autumn breeze shakes
    the trees causing the leaves
      to take flight looking like a
        billion bats flying into the
          night as the moon holds still in
            its place while the clouds roll
              by as if being chased, oh how
            beautiful it looks and how
          soothing the chill feels
        across the skin, the last
      season of the year, just
    before it ends, for I
  do solemnly swear
to catch an autumn breeze is very rare.

March 8, 2010

Flawless

Perfection
   was never the question,
but
 Flaws causes insurrection.
Creating problems of all kinds
   within the mind,
         because
Flaws is not the problem, it's
 the way we try to solve them.
Flaws don't define us,
    it only causes us to redefine
our true selves.
    So forget not and
      judge not. For everything
that has been or will be
    created is perfect for a purpose
and nothing that exists is
        worthless.

August 23, 2017

The Hustle Of A Lifetime

Never will you ever
find a hustle quite
like mine. I hustle
thoughts from the mind,
not nickels or dimes. I
entertain like dice entice
gamblers, sips of vodka on the
rocks the mind scrambler. In
this game hustles live or die,
clever as the devil or King
Solomon wise on closed eyes.
Nothing, but the truth no lie, just
another hustler on the rise.

November 1, 2017

The Life of a Clown

Happy they may
or may not be, but
this is the only reality
that we see.
Never considering
their sanity, loved ones
or family. The
paint is just a disguise
that hides what they're
really feeling inside.
Their clothes of old
shows no true perception,
only a dull reflection
of acceptance. When
things are put away
at the end of each day,
it's the smile on a child's face
that reminds them that
their life is not a waste.

November 1, 2017

We

We see
what we want to see,
Be what
we want to be and
believe
what we want to believe.
We hate, we love,
we discriminate, we judge,
we give, we take, we kill,
we create, we destroy,
we rebuild, we hurt,
we heal, we idolize,
we demoralize, we laugh,
we cry, we lie
then we die.

March 9, 2017

Rude Awakening

They say it's
 a thin line between
  love and hate,
   but what about fate or mistake
    or small and great, it's all open
     for debate.
The good, the bad, the
 happy and the sad, it's all
  one of the same. So, what is life
   aim if perceptions don't mean a
    thing that come and go like rain
     surrounded by clouds of question
      marks. Creating spots of ignorance
       in our intelligence for our presence
        is a limited existence, where
         death is always consistent.
Then you die
 is it all irrelevant
 if so, why?

October 29, 2017

Never Free

The reality of freedom
   can't be felt through the physical,
but only tasted through the sweet
   reality of the spiritual.
The pivotal understanding of
   our existence that constantly
meets resistance,
   causing wars of all kinds.
Fighting and fighting
   trying to break free,
just to be blind-sided
   by the reality of having
this body.

November 13, 2017

Divide and Conquer

Woe
to the generations
that will come
and go.
For many
will fall victim
to this foe.
It only takes
a second to have
you second-guessing
and believing
in a misconception.
Where a lie
is commonly accepted,
the truth is usually
rejected
and
in most cases never
corrected.

November 9, 2017

NoneTheLess

Seasons change for nothing remains the same, the reason being nature will explain. Death will come and life will go, rain will fall and rivers will flow. Nights plus days become decades as hairs of color turns gray and simply falls away, but nonetheless life still ends as it begins with only a breath.

November 7, 2017

The Seven Levels of Consciousness

My mind
is like a large room
with seven doors and
each one being a mystery
 out of its own curiosity.
   Where one of the seven was the
     entry, but which one I have no
       memory. As I paced the floor,
         I touched the knobs of each door
           looking for a sign of any kind
         before I realized that my mind
       was playing tricks. For where
     there was seven doors is now
   only six. The reality was
 simple, I had already
walked through it.

November 17, 2017

Day After Day

Each day begins
when the sun ascends,
raising the heat by degrees.
While shining its light along the
surface just to see a new day of
nature birthing, where the decent is
just as relevant. When the day light
begins to decline losing its shine as
darkness creeps into night and
begins casting shadows along
the way, the closing of
another day.

November 19, 2017

The Crime Scene

Crime happens all the time, but when you
see the yellow tape it's a sign that someone
             has died.

For some strange reason, it gives you an eerie
feeling of grief and sorrow in knowing
the victim won't be around tomorrow.

People start gathering in crowds, some whispering,
others screaming out loud
like they're in pain with tears running down
their faces as the police try to hold them back
from breaking through the tape.

They are usually the family or friends of the one
who died and so the police take them aside,
asking questions of "who, what, and why."

All you can hear are police sirens, along with
the screeching of tires as they brake or accelerate,
leaving behind black streaks in the street.

For that sound alone will shake you as the
smell of burnt rubber overtakes you.
Detectives are questioning potential witnesses,
trying to get a description of the guilty.

Yet you see no ambulance, only a van
of dark color pulls up with letters painted
             in yellow.

The coroner checks the victim's wallet

to see if he is a donor,
while organ transplant team awaits
the word from the coroner.

Then the forensic team searches the crime scene,
dusting for prints, with the constant clicking sound
of the camera taking shots of the blood spots,
outlining the splatters that seem to be
everywhere, giving off an odor of protein in the air.

The lifeless lump of dead flesh lies awkwardly,
face down, covered in blood,
beaten to death with a club.

The stick is still lying near the victim,
Making it easy to identify
What was used to kill him.

Like an art, they outline the body in chalk
before placing it in a black bag,
along with a name tag, before rolling it away
              on a cart.

The last you will see is the hand
pushing it into the van.

Then slowly the crowd starts to disperse,
for they have seen the worst,
as the body was carried away
              in a modern-day hearse.

Meanwhile, the tape is being removed with a few
still lingering, trying to see
where the body used to be.

Some even take a peek through the window,
*   trying to figure out the mystery before*
*   they leave*
with only a passing thought of another crime scene.

Real Men Cry, Too

It's said that real men don't cry, but that's a lie.
In the eyes of many it's considered a weakness,
but to me it's meekness
in its purest form,
as sugar is to water
when it's warm.

For I have cried many nights,
(not publicly, but out of sight).
Then tears ran down my face like rain;
I'm not a machine – I do feel pain.

How can a man use his power of expression
if he can't cry? Yet it's all right to do it
for someone who's died – and feeling anger
is highly expected, even accepted,
but to cry one must hide
because it's rejected.

Not to cry is pretending,
a fictional ending,
but for me it's a new beginning,
for when I cry it bring me relief,
giving me peace, not grief.

So when you see me cry
now you know why.
For I will no longer hide
what I feel inside – my emotions
make me know I'm alive!

And as for that myth,

*it's not true-
'cause real men cry,
too. Yes, we do!*

Aging Gracefully

The process of aging is so amazing
 to see babies grow well into their eighties.
It's a shame people don't respect it
 more, they rather stay young that's what
they really adore.
People have become so obsessed with staying
 young, they realize not what they have done.
Aging is natural and that's how it's
 supposed to be, but the world makes it seem ugly.
My dream is to live as long as I can,
 even older than the sand on beaches.
I want my skin to become so soft that
 it feels like cloth and my eyes would be
filled with zest showing my love for
 this quest.
I want all of my hair to turn gray and
 watch my great, great grandchildren play as
I sit on the porch and rock my day away.
There is beauty in growing old, it's like
 watching a story unfold or like wine it gets
better with time.
So, when you see the elderly treat them like
 kings and queens with respect and dignity.
They should be at the center of the
 world for they are more precious than any
diamond or pearl, but we treat
 material things better than life and you
know that ain't right.
The world neglects them and rejects them
 like they're already dead, but from past lives
they find time to make statues out of
 hot lead.

So, I can imagine how they feel inside,
 probably can't wait until the day they die.
But I, I admire your patience and
 virtues, it represents the past events
and everything you been through and
 your mind which is from an ancient time.
Your life is no mystery, rather it's
 a living history filled with knowledge and
wisdom, and only if we listen we might
 learn what we're really missing.
So, keep on keeping on as you age for
 each day of your life is like a page in a book
written in gold ink, keeping me in touch
 with something I love so much and that
is the key to aging gracefully.

I Am Not Just A Man

For you only see the color of my skin
And yes, I am a Afrikan.
But you see not what lies within
And I'm not speaking about my heritage.

For that has its own place in history
that's not all bloodshed and misery,
but was once a treasury until the
21st century.
No love for the land it's now all
about the money of man.

So, please forgive me if I sound cruel,
but in my heart is where truth rule.

For I stand before the world as I
came into it.
Naked, beaten and rejected, then to
die and never be resurrected.

In my earlier days of life
my face was twice as nice and
more pleasant to the sight.
But the wear and tear took its
toll on my flesh that stretch me
like a rubber band shaping me
to be this man.

Therefore, judge me not by what you
see, but by the quality of my
personality that reflects reality.

The essence of my core is the presence
of God, the crescent of my existence
that has brought me thus far that
some call Allah.

I can not describe what my eyes
have seen, but the man part is less
than a quarter of me. For I have seen
my true self in many dreams without
a body or extremities.

I appear as many like grains of sand
an hour glass that turns over time and
time again. As the words of "I am not
just a man" whistles in the wind,
constantly reminding me again and again.

Tears

Like effervescent bubbles when they
flow, so do tears when they come
and go.

It is purely a matter of expression
based on our emotional state, no matter
how small or great it happens anyway.

The body expresses itself through tears,
when we're happy, sad or suffering from fear.

Tears are very real, you can't fake the
way you feel.

It's a phenomenon within itself, how
these tiny drops express itself.

The eyes become like clouds when it rains,
pouring out water all the same, a gift from God
that words can't explain.

Each drop possesses a power of its own,
like an art gallery of pictures being shown.

They speak no words or even make
a sound as they shimmer down the
face as if in a race, each one traveling
at its own pace.

While reflecting a crystal clear light
along the way, as if to say we are
here to stay.

We shed so many tears in this life we live, but the eyes don't lie. So, when I cry it lets me know that I'm still alive!

MICHAEL WAYNE BRYANT

My Definition of Music

Imagine the size of a symphony
to produce every sound in the world,
combined together to each play a part
in perfect harmony
like ebony and ivory.

What time and effort it would take
to make something so wonderful and
great.

A task that the average person wouldn't
even contemplate or rather a mistake
to even try. A feat on the brink of
impossibility, anything else would be
a lie.

Yet, I can't deny what I feel inside
or envision from my third eye to create
the greatest ever composition.

By taking sound and cutting it to
such a precision to formulate a
musical catalyst from just one
note is beyond fabulous it's
miraculous.

A sound expressing musical tones
with baritones and microphones,
sending simulating vibrations
through your flesh down to your bones.

Elevating your soul beyond time and space,

causing your whole body to tremble and shake.
A feeling you will welcome with open arms,
mesmerized by its tantalizing charm.

As you find yourself levitating, while floating
like a cloud surrounded by musical notes
dancing and singing out loud.

Now, you're in a state of complete bliss,
while feeling weightless. So astonished
that such a creation should have never been
formulated, much less even written; but
outlawed and forbidden.

And like a pendulum being gravity stricken
this is God given with a touch of acoustics
is how I do it when I create
something called music!

Dazzled By A Poet

I put words together like a
chemist coming up with formulas
that will get you on the edge of your
seat, squirming and crossing your feet
in a state of anxiety.

Taking you to the pinnacle of anticipation,
where you're about to explode, because
you're losing patience and want to know.

You try to deny what you're feeling
and what your eyes are seeing.
An unbelievable arrangement of words
that can change your whole world with
just one glance and sharper than the
edge of a warrior's lance.

On the brink of ecstasy, a high
like you never felt before that will
lure you like a magic trick magnetized
by its movement.

As you try to shake it, but
you can't break its grip, because
you're on a mental trip.

To a placed you never been before
that you adore more and more as
you continue to read, causing your
heart to sing and your soul to bleed.

Like a spiritual journey beyond reality

in something called virtual reality.

Where your five senses no longer exist,
nothing, but complete darkness in the
wake of unconsciousness.

Like spontaneous combustion
rushing to the forefront of your
every thought.

Then, suddenly here comes a tiny
spark the size of a penny shining bright
in a shimmering light captivating you
in its glare.

As it gets closer and bigger
then mysteriously disappearing into
thin air like it was never there.

Then, you awaken staring at this piece
of paper with words written in ink
by me.

Rattled, because you just been dazzled
by a poet and didn't even know it.

I AM

I am whatever you want me to be
   your strength, your power or your integrity.
I am the good, the bad and the ugly,
   believing in me will give you peace for eternity.
I am the water you drink and the
   mind that causes you to think.
I am the one who put the world into
   motion and gave you feelings called emotions.
I am the sun, the moon and the stars
   and the one who gave the knowledge to come
   thus far.
I am not only the earth, but the entire
   universe some say you were last, but I tell
   you that you were first.
I am the wind that blows across your
   skin, the beginning and the end.
I am every religion and belief, and that
   which you can and cannot see.
I am the black, the white, the brown
   and the yellow wrapped up in each other.
I am every race, face and place, all
   that you see and everything work in harmony
   according to me.
I am the ocean, the sea and the
   land beneath your feet; and the sand
   and the dirt that makes everything work.
I am the plants and the trees that
   give off oxygen which allows you to breathe.
I am the right and the wrong, that which
   allows you to be weak or strong.
I am every animal and insect, so
   give nature its due respect.

I am the light, the truth and the way,
   unless through me there is no other way.
I am death and life.
I am your soul as well as the source
   to your existence.
I am the real without pretending.
I am the author of everything.
I am one with myself which means
   there is no one else and pure love like
   you have never felt.
I am the Alpha and Omega, and yes
   the one and only Creator who is consistently
   recreating myself in everything.
Therefore, there is no you, but only me for
   infinity.

MICHAEL WAYNE BRYANT

Flame On Me

I don't know what it is, but
  the way I feel is very real
Sometimes I seek you out and sometimes
  you elude me, causing mixed feelings
    that confuse me.
It's like a love-hate relationship.
No goodbye, no kiss, you just
  disappear into the harbor mist.
My heart aches just to be near
  you and my skin burns from
    your touch.
Your smell is unique as your body
  sway back and forth so eloquently.
I watch you from a distance as you
    dance putting me into a trace
      and your beauty captivates my
        every breath as I get closer
          with every step.
Fixation causes my eyes not to
  blink and clouds my mind to
    the point where I can't think.
I become emotionally stagnated
  as I stand before you with
    perspiration rolling down my face
      and a loss for words to say.
You seem to be angered by my presence
  and lash out like a harlot on a
    chariot.
Then suddenly, the winds begin to
  blow causing your moment to
    slow as you reach out to say
      goodbye before you go, filling

the skies with smoke.
You still remain, but not hardly the same
belittled to a glitter by the rain.
Now, you look like a silhouette with
a lit candle behind it, flickering
out so small I'm straining
my eyes just to find it.
I stare in disbelief as you disappear
into thin air leaving only a shadow
of your figure where you used to
be amongst the burnt leaves
and fallen trees.
My tears sizzle as it makes contact
with the ground, a sound telling
me that you will no longer be around.
The memories of you I will never
forget, because my heart still
burns with your love and
desire that inspire
me all the same never to forget
your name – flame.

The Forces That Be

I like the way the sun sneaks upon you
    at the break of dawn;
evaporating the dew on the grass and the
condensation that builds upon the glass
    with its radiance permeating the
    entire room from your body heat
    as you sleep,
    with each heartbeat,
    every breath rising in a 98.6 degree
    heat as you lie between the sheets.

I like the clouds whether moving or still;
    sometimes they seem so close I
    can reach out and feel their softness
    as they float through the sky
    like smoke to the human eye,
    forming different shapes
    that make me think
of God drawing pictures without a pencil or ink.

I like the rain that forms in its belly,
    building up like a volcano until
    it erupts bringing light or heavy drops
    as it hits the ground
    covering every dry spot leaving no
    rocks unturned and giving the
earth something it well deserves.

And what about those trees that stand like
    soldiers at ease,
    what is there not to like in such
    a beautiful delight that blocks

out the sunlight for the small creatures
that are sensitive to light and only
come out at night.
Its branches reaching out like a thousand
arms covered in leaves making a home for the
birds and bees.

I like the ocean and how it breaks down
in many degrees, forming rivers,
lakes and streams.
Sending water throughout the earth as it quenches
humanity's thirst.

I like the flowers and their variety in
many different colors and shapes,
giving off fragrances to satisfy any
taste with a look that will stagnate
you in one place.
Who? but God could have created such a gift.
Something with its pure presence that
can uplift with one sniff, and so sweet
it's like honey to the lips.

I like the thunder that roars like a lion in
a jungle and its partner called lighting that
can be quite frightening.
As the both of them can captivate your
mind sending static electricity up
your spine,
with its sound and sight a combination
that explodes like dynamite reaching
down to your soul giving humanity the
clear notion that there is a God,
However, close or far its presence leaves a
mental scar.

MICHAEL WAYNE BRYANT

The Transition

First, came the kiss then a little
 bit of that and a little bit of this.
Now, her last period she missed, a
 situation getting serious.

It started out all fun, now she going
 to have a son.
As the months passed her body weight
 increased as the little bundle of
life formed in her stomach with a heartbeat.

The ultrasound showed that he's well intact,
 while curled up within the embryo sack.
Complete formation without any complication.
 Lamaze class, hungry all the time and unable
to fast.

The time was near and four weeks later it
 was finally here.
Her water broke as the uterus dilated to 9cm
 makes way for the fetus to be born.
She began pushing and screaming, while
 sweat was streaming down her face
as her voice echoed throughout the whole
 place.

Then, suddenly the embryo sack rips
 as her hips shift making way for this
little beautiful gift.
 So small and so precious.

Not making a sound as the doctor turns

him upside down with a smack on
his backside, the baby begins to cry letting
the whole word know he's alive.

The mother cradles her child in her hands,
knowing that one day he will become a man.
As he sucks from her breast to feed, she wonders
what he will grow up to be.

From an infant to a toddler, the process of life
takes its course as he begins to develop
a voice.
No more crawling, just a lot of falling
as he begins to walk and talk.

His five senses begin to increase as
he continues to grow along with the
flow of information being created in his
brain.

Functioning swiftly and quickly, scrambling
to retain, while forming mental pictures
with the mixture of words this child begins
to learn.

From a firm environment and family structure,
which becomes his building blocks for
construction.

The mother will teach him how to be sensitive,
loving and caring as the father's time
comes near to rear him into manhood.

Then he leaves home fully grown to be on
his own, with tools he will use for

right or wrong.
He will set his goals high or low
and as time passes his mind will
continue to grow.
God will become a part of his life,
but how much depends on his
spiritual insight.

Then, the time will come for him to have
children, whether girl or boy they
will bring him joy.

Feeling proud with a sense of pride
as he looks into their eyes, a
moment he will never forget until the
day he dies.

Rejuvenation

Life isn't always as we predicted
and personal growth sometimes
becomes restricted causing
dedication to lead to frustration
a lost sense of patience.

Then comes anger and anxiety breaking
you down to depression leaving your
future in question as you hang in the
balance making your will to live a
real challenge.

Now take five deep breaths through
your nose expanding your diaphragm
while exhaling from your mouth sending
oxygen throughout your body north to
south with a sensation of energy
that increase as it's being released
calming you in peace.

Then return back to world feeling
your best, refreshed and ready to
finish life's quest.

IF

If I was a bird,
I would fly around the world.
If I was a jewel,
I would be a pearl so I could hide
beneath the sea where no one would find me.
If I was a clock, I would change
back the hands of time at least 3/5's
of my life just to make things right.
If I was the President, everyone
would have a place of residence.
If it wasn't for greed, jealousy
and envy people would live way past
a century.
If it wasn't for money, there would
be no banks.
If it wasn't for ink this paper
would still be blank, because I couldn't
write what I think.
If it wasn't for the female,
no one would be here.
If it wasn't for the sperm of man,
the whole world would be a deserted
land, because together they work hand in hand.
If it wasn't for guns, people
wouldn't get shot.
If it wasn't for crime,
you wouldn't be a cop.
If it wasn't for oxygen,
you couldn't breathe.
If it wasn't for death,
there wouldn't be any cemeteries.
If it wasn't for water,

you would die of thirst.
If you hadn't slipped,
you would have came in first.
If it wasn't for food,
the body would deteriorate.
If it wasn't for the love of meat,
there wouldn't be any drugs used to
make the animals grow more quickly.
If it wasn't for the chemicals, there
wouldn't be any pollution or the need
for scientists to come up with a solution.
If it wasn't for wars, mass killings
would cease.
If it wasn't for the militaries, there
wouldn't be any countries with armories
full of weapons with nuclear
capabilities.
If it wasn't for the laws,
nothing would be considered a crime.
If it wasn't for prisons,
nobody would be confined.
If everybody was color blind,
there wouldn't be a color line
and you wouldn't have to fight for
your rights or be judged on sight.
If it wasn't for airplanes and
boats, you couldn't travel coast to coast
and no need for passports, because
there wouldn't be nowhere to go.
If it wasn't for the belief in God,
there would be no faith or the need
for religions to show you the way.
If it wasn't for love, everybody
would hate, in a world created in chaos
that no one could escape.

*If it wasn't for common sense,
this poem would have never begun
much less ever end.
"If" is theoretically speaking
on what could have been or what
could happen.
Real life is not based on "If".
Whatever happens is because you created
it.
Therefore, make wise choices or you
will be hearing those same voices.*

I Need A Woman

I need a woman who will stick
 with me through thick or thin, not
  just a lover but also my best friend.
I need a woman with a vision sharpened
 to precision never quick in making decisions
  but embellished with a desire to rise
   higher that I can admire.
I need a woman who lives on honesty
 with an admiration for dedication without
  stipulations from past relations.
I need a woman with creativity and knows
 how to be happy without the presence of
  money or fame in search of something just to gain.
I need a woman with a heart of gold that
 loves God with all her soul with a divine
  essence that shines so bright it illuminates
   the night.
I need a woman who will push me to do my
 best and lay her head on my chest when she needs
  rest, so I can whisper sweet words in her ear
   letting her know how much I care.
I need a woman who will truly love me
 for me without the use of larceny.
I need a woman who wants to be
 my queen for a king with a burning
  passion and together we can make miracles
   happen.
I need a woman that will stand by her
 man hand in hand with style and grace
  with a touch of seduction to keep the wood
   burning in the fireplace.
I need a woman with a foundation in
 faithfulness and trust, and for every man
  a woman is a must.

The Death of a Flower

  Liquidated by the rain that nurture this earth, she feels as though she no longer has any worth, but is cursed by the lord of time yet she still stands and blooms like an ancient shrine
  The first and last of her kind, beautiful and divine, preserved like the best of wine that survive by her roots not by a vine
  With that in mind she knows not her holy design and decline to take her rightful place.
  A lost flower desecrated by the hands of her own mate and seed's she can no longer germinate, defiled and corrupted by humanity she suffers from insanity.
  Inching closer and closer to her final hour, the death of a flower

July 21, 2017

The Pen and Paper Part 2

The pen and paper was the first part,
Now, I'm giving you what created this art.
Its throne sets on the paper, and
the scepter is the pen, but nothing begins
without the commands of its demands.
With a twist of the risk,
it becomes mystic,
performing magic like it was artistic,
with a style that's unconventional while
rearranging words to make it sensual,
impenetrable like three dimensional.
From a dream to a story theme,
back to reality as it leaves the scene.
Raising your self-esteem,
No residue of its presence only crystal clean.
I gave you the visual,
Now, it's time for the pivotal in this
immortal ritual.
It's greatness in the making,
but it is nothing without the pen and paper.
Yet, it stands alone, because it's able
as it lies dormant on the table.
And as the sun rise and sets at night
it comes to life and takes flight.
To liquidate the paper with ink,
as it formulates words to make you think.
Turning a screenplay into motion picture,
while forming characters out of its own literature.
Its dominance is of a king,
so say hello to the rated supreme.
More faster than the speed of light, to
rest itself in the Harlem night.

Not to speak verbally, but mentally
as it stands like the Statue of Liberty.
For its movements is dramatic, but
still systematic that generate static to
electricity giving it simplicity to write
out history.
From a duet to a trio, it became and will
remain in its own domain.
As it continues to marvel and excel the human
mind time and time again,
Throughout the land, because you have
witness the power of the hand.

September 4, 2007

Saying Goodbye

Your death was a terrible time
for me those memories still
 haunt me.
 So many questions, but little
answers that ate me up like cancer.
 I became emotionally and
mentally incapacitated, so
 devastated that I became isolated.
 It was too quick and sudden,
I never had the chance to tell you
 how much I really loved you.
 To me that's the biggest part
when a loved one suddenly departs.
 In a blink of an eye
somebody dies and you never have
 the chance to say goodbye!

October 31, 2006

MICHAEL WAYNE BRYANT

No Proof of Life

Mouth gagged
so I can't scream,
alive or dead I might
be. Wrist and ankles
bound with tape, face
down on a metal plate,
scared, cold and blindfold.
Whispers of a light conversation,
hands and feet numb from the lack
of blood circulation, filled with anxiety,
somebody please talk to me. A hostage
situation, police central command
awaits patiently as the family
looks on anxiously, but the
call never comes.

February 22, 2016

Wake-Up

Wake-up,
because I'm just trying to
get you to see that you're
mentally asleep making your
reality nothing more than foolery.
Wake-up,
Before time seals your fate
for the truth is solid, where
lies crack then break.
So please wake-up,
because fools can't be
convinced. Now it's
your turn to exit the pool
of foolishness
or continue to swim
in the bliss of ignorance.

September 20, 2016

The Crime

When a crime has been
committed, yellow tape marks off
the crime scene no one admitted.
The first on the scene
is the forensic team, who outline
the body in chalk.
Then pictures are taken
in the dark under ultraviolet
lights making physical evidence
more visible to sight.
Color coded cards with numbers
mark off the blood spots, click, click
more camera shots as
white sheets soaked in red
stains cover the dead remains.
Then the coroner enters
and make his claim, but the
real question is who would
do such a thing.

September 23, 2016

Promises

All of us make them but without loyalty
 makes it easy to break them.
I take it very serious from the start in giving
 my word from the heart.
I don't make promises like wishes just
 to give hope then turn around and cut
    the rope.
Some fake it just to be part of something
 when their true intention is to do nothing.
They fail to realize the damage they have
 done and laugh about it as if it's
    fun.
It never means much then until you get
 the tail end then laughter suddenly
    becomes concern because you been
       burned.
Yet in reality it's a hard way to learn
 but you get what you deserve and
    as the old cliché goes, what goes
       around comes around.
So, in giving your word be willing to live
 it with honor and self-respect making
it the main subject in your curriculum
of life, a trait of someone striving
 to do right.
Some promises can't be kept and
 usually heartfelt, but things happen
beyond our control and that's how
 life goes.
So just play the hand that you were
 dealt and never fold, because
keeping one's promise should be
 one's goal which is worth more
than a ton of gold.

Rhythm of the Rhyme

Sour like a lemon or lime, but sweet like honeycomb
dripping from every line that's the rhythm
of the rhyme filled with words that will
creep up on you from behind to play hide
and seek with your mind to be
consumed by the fumes of ink writing
out such a masterpiece that will
make you think as you sink into your
own essence like a crescent of a
moon in the middle of the night
and watch the words develop
wings to take flight just to see
them settle upon your heart
is a work of art that soothes
your soul and carries away
woes like a push cart, as
promised it delivers like an
homage without a word
spoken the rhythm of
the rhyme keeps on
stroking like a
magical potion flowing
through the air in slow
motion.

May 6, 2015

I Remember Now

If
there's no such thing as death and my
 flesh and bones are truly not alive,
 then tell me why I try so hard
not to die and if this is true then
 everything else about life might be a
 lie too,
making me not really me and you
 not really you, like fictional
characters in the play of the mind,
 for it is written that I am
 a soul of divinity, but
spiritually blind with no
 memory of my holy ancestry, lost
 and confined to space and
time. Yet, in the pit of my stomach
 I do feel something that I cannot
 comprehend, it's like a fire burning
from within, a sensation of flames
 thrusting from the top of my head as
beams of bright lights burst from the
 cracks in my skin, is this the
beginning of the end or the truth being
born again.

August 28, 2016

About the Author

I am presently incarcerated and have been since 1988 at the age of 18. My claims of innocence have never interested those in authority, nor raise an eyebrow in the name of justice. It's true, "You can't judge a book by it's cover", but many do and I guess that's why I'm still incarcerated. Nevertheless, I continue to endure spiritually, grow mentally and stay strong physically. My foundation has always been the concept of spirit, mind, and body. The balance I longed for that resulted in…

```
              The
          M  POS MEN  T
        O              I
      C                  S
```

www.ingramcontent.com/pod-product-compliance
Lightning Source LLC
Chambersburg PA
CBHW081354070526
44583CB00020B/2550